# MORE MEMORIES
## OF
# SHEFFIELD

TRUE NORTH BOOKS
ELLAND
HALIFAX
WEST YORKSHIRE
HX5 9AE
TEL 01422 377977

C000076637

THE PUBLISHERS WOULD LIKE TO THANK THE
FOLLOWING COMPANIES FOR SUPPORTING THE
PRODUCTION OF THIS BOOK

MAIN SPONSOR

## RJ STOKES & COMPANY LIMITED

ARKOTE LIMITED

ATKINSON WALKER (SAWS) LIMITED

BAKER BLOWER ENGINEERING LIMITED

BROWNILL VICKERS

DORMER TOOLS (SHEFFIELD) LIMITED

FLETCHERS BAKERIES LIMITED

CW FLETCHER & SONS LIMITED

GREENUP PACKAGING LIMITED

ERNEST H HILL LIMITED

LAND INSTRUMENTS INTERNATIONAL LIMITED

MARSDENS CATERERS OF SHEFFIELD LIMITED

H PONSFORD LIMITED

SHEFFLEX LIMITED

THORNTONS PLC

WILLIAMS FASTENERS

First published in Great Britain by True North Books
Elland
Halifax  HX5 9AE
1998

ISBN 1 900 463 32 6

# Introduction

The publication of our first book, *Memories of Sheffield* met with a tremendous response from the people in the city. Thousands of copies of the original book have been sold to date, with many finding their way overseas to bring pleasure to former Sheffield residents who had emigrated. The letters of encouragement and kind comments we received urged us to produce a second book, this time containing even more of the excellent photographs which had provided such enjoyment. The compilation of *More Memories of Sheffield* has been carried out over a period of several months. We always expected it to be a pleasurable experience, but in the event the satisfaction we have derived from studying the marvellous old photographs went far beyond our expectations.

Increasingly, *nostalgia* is enjoyed by a growing band of people and the book is intended to appeal to a wide audience. Where possible we have tried to concentrate upon a period within the memory of most of our readers; the 1940s, 50s and 60s - decades which saw tremendous changes in the city, and a time when changes in the world of work, entertainment, public health and retailing. *Change* takes place constantly in every city and Sheffield is no exception. As we all get older it is often easier to 'step back' and view events and developments with a clearer sense of perspective. Our aim has been to assist in this respect by presenting a 'catalyst' capable of rekindling memories of days gone by in an entertaining manner.

Looking through the pages of this book it may be surprising how much change has taken place, and over such a relatively short period, relative to the long history of the area. Several of Sheffield's best known and longest established firms have allowed us access to their often extensive internal archives. This has enabled us to recount the history of these companies, from humble beginnings to, in most cases, leading positions in their chosen area of expertise. Of course, these organisations have tremendous social, as well as commercial significance, as between them they represent the places of employment for thousand upon thousand Sheffield people. We are grateful for the co-operation and support of the directors of these businesses for adding to the quality and interest of this book.

Many of the children featured in these photographs will be reaching retirement age now and we would be pleased to hear from anyone who may have recognised themselves.

Street scenes are not neglected. Photographs of this nature were popular in the last book, and understandably so. The changing face of the city is reflected in the way our roads and shops have developed to meet the changing needs of our lives over the years. These photographs show the shops and motorcars we remember from our early days, along with the fashions which were all the rage when we were younger. All combine to refresh our memories of days gone by, and when that occurs the book will have achieved its aim.

We hope that you enjoy reading *More Memories of Sheffield* as much as we enjoyed creating it.

PHOTOGRAPH COMPILATION/COVER DESIGN.........................................MARK SMITH

CAPTION RESEARCH AND COMPILATION...........................................PEGGY BURNS

DESIGNERS...................MANDY WALKER, NICKY BRIGHTON AND CHRISTINE GALE

COPYWRITER...............................................................................PAULINE BELL

BUSINESS DEVELOPMENT EDITOR................................................GARETH MARTIN

# CONTENTS

# Around the city centre

Though Fargate has been pedestrianised and the shops have changed, the well loved shopping street is still recognisable from this photograph taken in 1950. The Town Hall stands out proudly against the sky. The shops pictured here will still be familiar to many readers: Atkinson's Fargate store, T C Palmers, Etams, and possibly the most famous of them all, Cole Brothers store, off to the right of the picture. 'I'll see you on Cole's corner,' was the sentence that arranged hundreds of meetings and sparked off many a romantic attachment.

The interior of Coles' store is worth mentioning for nostalgia's sake - one could even describe it as rather quaint, with goods laid out in interconnecting rooms rather than in the large halls that became the accepted type of layout in the majority of department stores. The singular layout, however, would have made converting the store to the number of small business that have taken over the building today an easy matter. Sheffield's popular Marks and Spencers store is to the left of the photograph.

**Above:** Sheffield's scars were gradually fading as the city's rebuilding and renovation work went on, and here and there advertising hoardings helped to disguise the worst of the ravages. This one, on the corner of Flat Street and Pond Hill, was well placed near the Post Office and the bus station; perhaps some of the people in this photograph were tempted by the tall dark glass of Guinness and dropped in for a quick drink at the local on the way home. The British public have believed that Guinness was good for them since the drink was first advertised in 1929. When they decided to advertise, Arthur Guinness & Son called in some consumer research experts to help them with the ads. The experts found that many of the punters believed it did them good - and the first Guinness slogan, 'Guinness is so Strengthening' was born. Many clever slogans have been produced over the years: 'Tall, Dark and Have Some', 'Seven Million Every Day and Still Going Down' and notably 'I've Never Tried it Because I Don't Like it'. And remember 'Guinness is Good for you - Just think what Toucan do'?

**Above right:** Where did they all go to? Police officers on point duty, that is. There was a time when every major junction in every major town had its traffic bobby; remember those black and white zebra-striped boxes they used to use? The boxes made them highly visible and gave them the air of authority they needed. A few at a time they departed, leaving the motorist with a legacy of traffic lights to contend with at each junction. Traffic lights, while keeping the traffic flowing smoothly through the town centre somehow lack the personal touch provided by the good old British bobby.

These two police officers are directing traffic and pedestrians in Waingate back in 1946; there were plenty of people about on this rainy day, and there were plenty of buses and trams about too, so perhaps this was a busy Saturday afternoon, or the end of a working day. The scars of war can still be detected on the right, and a Jubilee Stout advert helps to disguise the bombed-out building. A shopping precinct would eventually be developed on the site. The buildings to the left have all disappeared now to make room for the new Court House.

*The familiar silhouette of the Town Hall and the elegant Cathedral spire grace the skyline in this photograph that dates from 1950. A keen eye might spot the crowds in the background; a sign board on the corner of the property advertises a 'Special Price Sale', and the occasion has obviously tempted Sheffielders to venture out in search of a bargain. Traffic still flows freely along the Moor in 1950, and Sheffield as a whole was affected by the post war increase in private transport. In 1938 there were 29,126 motor vehicles licenced in the city; by 1970 the figure had increased to 117,610. As traffic increased so did the number of accidents. The city responded by introducing traffic free areas, and the Moor was made into a pedestrianised area in 1979. The cleared bomb site to the left of the photograph bears witness to the enormous losses suffered in the Moor during the second world war.*

**Below:** The Burtons building on the corner of High Street and Angel Street took a real hammering from German bombs on the night of 12th December 1940, and a sign on the corner of the building here advises customers that their business has been transferred to Burtons at 20-22 Haymarket. The 1940 raid left little standing on the south side of High Street; the fine C&A Modes building next to Burtons - only eight years old - was completely gutted. C&A Modes was opened in 1932 on the site of the old Fitzalan Market which had served Sheffielders for an amazing 144 years when it was demolished in 1930. Little damage was done on the other side of High Street. This photograph was taken in 1952, and post-war reconstruction was well underway. Today's shoppers are more likely to connect the high class furnishings business Waring and Gillow with the old Burton building. High Street has long been the focus of change. During the 19th Century it was a very narrow thoroughfare, and even horse-drawn vehicles caused traffic jams at times. Old properties on both sides of the street were eventually demolished in a grand road widening scheme.

*A police officer on point duty adds that personal touch as he shepherds shoppers across the pedestrian crossing in High Street. As can be seen by the number of trams approaching Fargate, Sheffield has an excellent tradition when it comes to public transport. These pedestrians were caught on camera in April 1952. The building in the centre of the photograph is of course the former offices of the Sheffield Telegraph and Star, whose fine building with its distinctive clock tower is a familiar landmark in the city. In earlier years the Daily Telegraph had its home in a smaller building on the same site, and the illuminated sign mounted on its roof informed Sheffielders that a scarcely believable 1,250,000 copies of the newspaper were sold per week. The building, along with the two adjoining properties, one of which was Harvey Naylor's clothing store on the corner of York Street, was demolished in 1913. The city had two newspapers, the Telegraph and the Independent, and on 31st October 1938 the two papers amalgamated without prior warning, publishing the first copy of the Sheffield Telegraph and Daily Independent. Today The Star is Sheffield's only newspaper.*

**Above:** In 1905 Town Hall Square underwent another of its periodic changes, and the space that had formerly been occupied by the Jubilee Monolith was given over to a statue of Queen Victoria, its effect being somewhat spoiled by the rather forbidding iron railings that surrounded the statue. Those people who had been used to using the base of the Monolith as a seat would no doubt have been rather miffed. That landmark too had a short life; in 1930 Queen Victoria joined her Jubilee Monolith in Endcliffe Park. Four years later more changes were made and a rock garden gave a pleasant and less formal air to Town Hall Square. By the 1950s a simple roundabout had taken over. Fargate was pedestrianised in 1973 (though some drivers persisted in ignoring the restrictions). In 1961 Sir Stuart Goodwin, a local industrialist, presented the city with the fountain that was given his name. The Goodwin Fountain, its many jets spraying water high in the air, became a popular landmark. In 1998 the fountain was removed to the Peace Gardens.

**Above left:** Surrounded by scaffolding, the construction of Walsh's new store is well underway in this 1952 photograph. Older Sheffielders will remember Walsh's superb city department store as it was before the Blitz of 1940 turned it into a burnt-out shell. John Walsh built his famous store on the site previously occupied by Nicholson's Mart, and the High Street store quickly established a reputation for its range of quality fashions and furnishings, its orchestra and its pleasant restaurant. The new department store was completed by the following year and was opened in May 1953. The store later passed from Walsh's to Rackham's and in turn became House of Frazer. Today's Sheffielders shop at T J Hughes department store. Gerrards, whose sign advertised gowns, furs and mantles (a loosely fitting cloak or coat), was also badly damaged during the war and struggled on without the upper floors of the building. High Street today is virtually unrecognisable; modern buildings have now replaced the blitzed properties, and Arundel Gate sweeps across the area. A huge open-topped subway known to most as simply 'the hole in the road' was added to High Street and formally named Castle Square, appearing from above like a gigantic staring eye.

*Do you remember the 1960s illuminated Guinness advert atop Wallis's ladies' fashion shop that used to fascinate every youngster passing along Fargate after dark? The building has a long tradition of being occupied by tailors and fashion shops; as long ago as 1879 the premises were taken by Robert Hanbidge, who had a hat shop there. In 1941 Walsh's moved their store into the building - their earlier department store in High Street had been destroyed in the 1940 bombing raid. This particular site has an illustrious past; the Duke of Norfolk's home was here, built in 1711. Today Fargate is Sheffield's busiest pedestrian walkway, and in recent years natural stone paving has replaced the earlier concrete surface in Fargate and Norfolk Row. The area has been endowed with a continental look that Sheffielders have loved to hate. First of all the fact that Italian craftsmen were brought in to lay the decorative cobbles did not go down well, especially with the city's own pavers who understandably felt badly done-to. Another real bone of contention was the cobbles themselves, which proved to be uncomfortable to walk on and a teeth-rattling experience for wheelchair users.*

**Above:** Remember those days before double yellow lines? It is interesting to note that although little traffic apart from public transport is moving, unrestricted parking is allowed in Fargate. And traffic obviously flows in either direction, though because of the growth in popularity of the motor car a number of different experiments were made with one-way traffic through the city centre as early as 1930. This photograph was taken in 1952, and trams were still a popular form of transport in the city. It would be another eight years before they disappeared from the city streets. On the left of the photograph is Proctors furniture store, and more than a few Sheffield couples will be able to remember paying a little each week towards furniture for when they got married. By the time they tied the knot the happy couple would have enough in the kitty to buy furniture for their first home. Further down on the left is Coles' department store and the famous Coles' corner meeting place. Today, Coles' department store is opposite the City Hall in Barker's Pool.

**Right:** By 1963 a lot of changes had been made in Fargate. Many of the businesses and shops had been there for many years, but as can be seen by comparing this photograph with older ones, smart new modern shop fronts had brought shops such as Anne Lennard and Dr Scholls (who were holding a sale on the day this picture was taken) up to date. Others, such as the massive Table Waters sign by 'you know who', never seemed to change. Schweppes was responsible for a number of clever adverts. The company took advantage of the spy fever that was raging in the 1960s; the popular 'Danger Man' series and the new James Bond movies gave the advertisers the idea for the slogan 'What is the Secret of Schhh?'. The product did not even have to be named in the ad - a copywriter's dream - and though at one stage the company talked about inviting Patrick Magoohan, star of 'Danger Man', to do them, those 'you know who' adverts made William Franklyn, who acted in various spoof spy situations, familiar to every household that owned a TV set.

The bronze statue of King Edward VII stands impassively ubove the ladies and gents loos and the familiar red phone boxes from his pedestal in Fitzalan Square; he has the dubious privilege of being the only statue left in Sheffield city centre in the 1990s. The domed building in the background is of course the GPO. The White Building (here the premises of London and Lancashire Insurance) occupies a position on the right of the photograph; a surprising number of Sheffielders are still unaware of the relief decoration of men working in traditional Sheffield industries that embellishes the front of the building. The Marples Hotel, advertising Magnet Ales, was completed in 1959 and stands on the site of the older Marples. Another old landmark was the 'Cabman's Shelter', a circular structure which not only provided shelter to people waiting for trams but informed Sheffielders of the time in the early years of the 19th Century.

Fitzalan Square had two cinemas, the Electra Palace, which reopened at the end of the war in 1945 as the News Theatre and in 1962 went on to become the Classic, and the Odeon which stood on the corner of Flat Street.

**Above:** Looking towards Fitzalan Square, one can just pick out the dome of the GPO on the far left of the photograph, taken in 1964. In the centre is the statue of King Edward VII and to the Sovereign's right is the Odeon building, in 1964 still showing films. Musicals proved popular with the punters; 'South Pacific' ran for six months during 1958 and 'The Sound of Music' attracted picture-goers for an amazing two years, from 1965 to 1967. The Odeon became a bingo hall in June 1971. Haymarket was traditionally a popular place to shop and eat. John Collier menswear is on the right, as is the Brunswick Hotel which has now been replaced by a number of small shops. Davy's Restaurant is at the centre of the photograph, and over the years it had gone through a number of name changes; in 1961 it was Davy's Mikado Cafe, now three years on it advertises itself as the Quick 'n Twenty. The tudor-style building - sadly now gone - housed Proctor's furniture store, which many Sheffielders will remember; the sign in the window advises passers-by 'Proctor's for Finest Furniture'. Neville Reed, the well-known chain of menswear, is next door along.

**Above right:** The eye is drawn immediately to the central point of this 1960 photograph, where Castle Market is under construction in Waingate. The market opened in 1962, bringing to completion the Castle Market project - the first part was built as long ago as

1930. Castle Market proved to be immensely popular with shoppers, and virtually anything from the cheap and cheerful to the more stylish could be bought there. A bridge at second-storey height took pedestrians from Castle Market across Exchange Street to Woolworths. The building also housed a branch of the National Westminster Bank. The Royal Hotel, well known in the 19th Century as a terminus for the Attercliffe and Heeley horse omnibus service, was one of the buildings which once stood on the market site. Castle Market takes its name of course from Sheffield Castle, which occupied much of the area in more ancient times. (The castle was built in 1270.) Interestingly the drawbridge supports and part of one of the castle's gatehouse towers still exist below the foundations of the market.

**Above:** Plans were made to build a cinema in Flat Street as early as 1933, and a site was actually leased from the City Council. Work had already begun when war was declared in 1939, and by 1954, when restrictions on new constructions were removed, plans for the new city circle road scheme were already in hand. The partly-constructed Odeon, designed to seat 2,326, had to be demolished, and new plans were drawn up. The new cinema was the largest to be built in Britain since World War II, with seats for 1,524 in the stalls and 816 in the circle. A thousand yards of red flowered carpet was laid and a 55ft wide screen added which could be adjusted to meet any desired screen size or shape. This fascinating photograph was taken on the Gala Opening Day, 16 July 1956, and because the first film was 'Reach for the Sky' a contingent from RAF Norton attended the performance. Also there were the Deputy Lord Mayor, John Davis, Managing Director of the Rank Organisation and film star Dinah Sheridan. The cinema's last film was shown in June 1971 and it opened as a Bingo Hall the very next day.

**Below:** A Number 82 bus negotiates the roundabout at the Townhead Street and Broad Lane road junction in 1964. Today the roundabout has changed, but the surrounding buildings have changed little over the years. The garage on the left, here displaying a Shell sign, is still there, as is its competitor on the other side of the roundabout. Off to the right is Tenter Street and West Bar Green, now part of the inner ring road. Interestingly, it was from the nearby Tenter Street Depot that the procession of Sheffield's last trams left for their historic journey through the city at 6pm on 8th October 1960. To the immediate left is Townhead Street, and further around Broad Lane leaves the premises of DER to its right as it leads off in the direction of Weston Park and Crookesmoor Park. Weston Park, overlooked by the University's Arts Tower, is home to the City Museum and Mappin Art Gallery. The 19th Century museum contains the largest collection of Sheffield Plate in the world. Sheffield has long been known for its parks and open spaces; the city has more than 50 parks, and the number of trees has been estimated at four per person!

**Right:** Looking towards Fargate in 1969, and though sweeping changes had already been made in the city, the Legal and General building, facing us from across the road, was still the same. To the right of the photograph is, of course, the Town Hall which looked all the better for the addition of a few trees and pleasant tubs of flowers. The original site for the Town Hall was an area of crowded shops, pubs and houses, which were cleared to make way for the new municipal buildings. Designed by E W Mountford, the Town Hall was built mainly from stone quarried at Stoke Hall Quarry in Derbyshire, Queen Victoria herself travelled to Sheffield on 21st May 1897 to declare the new Town Hall officially open. A 21-gun salute greeted the arrival of the Royal Train, and large crowds cheered Her Majesty as she was driven to the Town Hall. Addresses were read, presentations made, and the Queen ceremonially unlocked the gates with a gold key. The figure of Vulcan, the Roman god of fire, still sits atop the 210ft tower, a symbol of the Steel City's traditional industry. Vulcan is also depicted on the city's coat of arms.

# *Putting a shine on Sheffield*

Robert James Stokes came rather reluctantly into the paint and varnish trade in 1887. In Wrexham, where his family lived, he had been making good money by delivering papers on a country round. When his father persuaded him to become apprenticed to J F Smith, a paint and varnish merchant of Yorke Street, Wrexham, the money was a severe blow to his personal pride. However, he realised that the training would be to his ultimate benefit.

In 1894 he worked very briefly for R R Minton & Company in Liverpool, before being sent to their branch shop in Leeds. The following year he was directed to open a new shop for them at 102, Norfolk Street, Sheffield.

He found Sheffield a friendly place. He joined Brunswick Wesleyan Chapel and there met with

*Above: Where it all started in Little London Street.*
*Below: Inside the factory on Little London Street.*
*Facing page: R.J Stokes & five brothers (R.J Stokes centre rear).*

great kindness from Mr James Lamb, the Sheffield draper. At the latter's home, he met Sabina Himsworth the future Mrs Stokes. They became engaged in 1897 but decided to delay their marriage until Robert had set up in business on his own account.

He achieved this goal in March 1899, in premises at 62, Cambridge Street, with the help of his brother Walter. By 1903 the Stokes were able to open a branch establishment in Packers Row, Chesterfield, which was managed by the eldest brother, Frank.

the accountants for R J Stokes to this day, although their current title is Wingfield, Slater & Hemingfield.

Three years later the Sheffield building had become too small and larger premises were built at 44, Cambridge Street. Here the business was hampered by

Having got his company running, Robert Stokes realised that he would need an accountant. He had been in business long enough to know that it was the people with plenty of work to do already who would be the most efficient workers. He therefore looked for a "busy man" and settled on a Mr Carnall of Carnall Slater. This firm are still

water that seeped into the basement, several times, flooding it to a depth of twelve inches. Stock was damaged and labour was wasted in pumping it out. It was not until some years later, when the Hippodrome was built next door, that the severed water pipe that had been causing the trouble was found and repaired.

As the firm grew, it absorbed more family members. Herbert George Stokes joined the

business in 1906. Robert Stokes bought a piece of land in Kingfield Road and built two houses on it, one for his wife's parents and one for his own family. In 1908 William Stokes joined the firm.

By 1913, business was flourishing to the extent that Robert could afford to buy the business of his late master at Yorke Street, Wrexham and William was sent to manage it for him. In Sheffield, Thomas Henry Stokes, generally known as 'Ern', came to work for the family company.

By 1915, a severe shortage of staff caused by recruitment into the armed forces at the outbreak of the First World War meant that Edwin Goddard Stokes, Robert's son had to leave

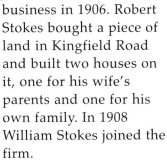

school and hold the fort in the business. This could not have been an easy task for a schoolboy, however many times he had heard his elders discussing the finer points of business practice. However, his own talents and the help of the staff left behind in Sheffield enabled him not only to cope but to lead the business forward.

After the war a piece of land was bought in Little London Road, Sheffield as a site for a works for the firm. Here, by June 1921, a paint mill and a varnish-making kitchen were completed. The firm was made into a limited company two years later, with Robert Stokes as Chairman and Managing director, and his brothers Walter and Frank and his son Edwin as life directors.

The paint trade was healthy so that, when Chesterfield town was being largely rebuilt, the firm built larger and more convenient premises in Knifesmith Gate, Chesterfield, whilst in Sheffield a range of varnish storehouses was added to the works in 1925.

*Above: Staff having a break in the sunshine outside the factory in the 1930's.*
*Facing page top: Close up of the barrels and water-pumps inside the factory at the beginning of the century.*
*Facing page bottom: Sitting in the sun with their flat caps on, the staff posing for their photo to be taken in the 1930's.*

In 1928 Robert Stokes wanted to expand his business in Wrexham. He bought premises to achieve this at 19 High Street. This was the year another of Robert's sons, Jim, joined the company. Robert built another house for himself in Kingfield Road, Sheffield and moved into it. He went on building, this time additional shop premises in Waingate, Sheffield, on the site of the moat of the old Sheffield Castle. Thomas Henry Stocks (Ern) went there to manage it.

Another retail outlet meant that more production capacity was needed at the works and so, in 1930, the paint mill was extended and fitted with

a large electric goods lift. Also, in 1933-34 the frontage to Little London Road was built up, giving the business a new paint mill, cellulose shop, garage and test room. Also, an additional storey was built over the premises in Cambridge Street.

In Rotherham a corner piece of land was bought on the main street, fronting Westgate and Ship Hill. Here five shops were built, one being occupied by R J Stokes & Company Limited. Suites of offices were built over all five shops and a dance hall over the offices.

At that time Robert stokes created R J S (Estates) Limited, a holding company for the various shop properties of the firm. The directorate was exactly the same as for the parent firm, with the addition of Jim Stokes, who by now had been elected a director of R J Stokes & Company Limited.

Another innovation was a Benevolent Trust Fund, created in February 1938 for the benefit of aged employees. A sum of money was voted from the company's funds as a nucleus and further sums were voted every year.

When war broke out again in 1939, many of the firm's employees were in the Territorials and so were called up immediately. Others followed until, eventually R J Stokes was scheduled under an 'Essential Works Order'. This, together with the fact that 90% of the firm's turnover then was for Government work, enabled them to keep the remainder of their staff. Stokes were appointed by the Air Ministry to manufacture paint for the camouflage schemes at the big steel works. They also supplied many Army and Air Force units as well as the American Army units that were stationed in the neighbourhood.

*Left:* R.J Stokes shop around the 1930's selling paint and wallpaper. Wallpaper was a luxury at one time. Was the writing on the window painted on.
*Below:* A sketch of 44 Cambridge Street.

By order of the Ministry of Supply, all private sales were stopped with the exception of those to be used for the repair of Blitz damage.

The works itself was hit by German bombs on the night of May 9th 1941. A terrific fire took hold and reached the archway before it was controlled and eventually quenched. By then, it had destroyed No 1 Paint Mill and the stockroom with all its contents. Robert Stokes was shocked but philosophical. He and son Edwin were at the builder's officers first thing the next morning to engage him in the rebuilding. Permission for this had to be obtained from the Emergency Reconstruction Panel of the Ministry of Supply which allocated labour and raw materials for

repairs according to their urgency. Rebuilding the Stokes' Works was achieved, complete with the installation of new machinery, in the space of six months. Unfortunately, only three years later a good deal of damage was done in a fire that broke out in the cellulose shop. Again the company was given high priority for repairs.

In 1946 a plan was made to extend the paint mill and build another alongside it but a building license was not made available to them until 1952. Even then it was another two years before materials and labour could be made available to finish the job and by then the pressure in the trade had passed and throughout the fifties competition in the paint industry was extremely keen.

Robert Stokes died peacefully from a heart condition in 1953 and Mr E G Stokes succeeded his as Chairman and Managing Director. His son, the second R J Stokes, became a director at the tender age of 21 and Chairman and joint managing Director in his turn, on the retirement of his father and the death of Mr J W B Stokes.

Mr C J Stokes was meanwhile made joint managing director responsible for paint manufacturing. Mrs Ann Stokes, who joined the company 25 years ago after completing a course in interior design, refers to herself as 'quite a newcomer'!

In the early seventies Mr R J Stokes junior expanded into the tile business which has now become the company's largest department. Tiles are imported from all over the world and distributed to retailers throughout the UK.

In the persons of Messrs T J Stokes, R C Stokes and J Stokes, the company is now entering its fourth generation of family management as it supplies the materials that keep Sheffield interiors well maintained and decorated.

*Above: How times have changed R.J Stokes today with transport ready for distribution.*
*Facing page top: A close up shot of staff outside the old factory*
*Facing page bottom: Incendiary bomb damage to the old factory during the Second World War.*

# Wartime

**Above:** Sir Anthony Eden, Secretary of State for War, appealed in a radio broadcast for men between 17 and 65 to make up a new force, the Local Defence Volunteers, to guard vulnerable points from possible Nazi attack. Within four minutes the first man was putting his name down at his local police station. By the next day long queues of volunteers had formed. At first the new force had to improvise; there were no weapons to spare and men had to rely on sticks, shotguns handed in by local people, and on sheer determination. Weapons and uniforms did not become available for several months. In July the Local Defence Volunteers became the Home Guard. The Guard posted sentries to watch for possible aircraft or parachute landings at likely spots such as the disused aerodrome at Norton, golf courses around the city, local parks and at Redmires racecourse. They manned anti-aircraft rocket guns, liaised with other units and with regular troops, set up communications and organised balloon barrages. The Hallamshire zone of the Home Guard included a special Post Office section, whose specialist knowledge was put to good use in cable laying.

**Inset:** During World War II Sheffield had 130 air raid alerts, and when the warning siren sounded it was time to fly the barrage balloons. Balloon barrages had been placed in the most important areas, and seventy-two sites around the city had been allocated for the balloons. Parks, recreation grounds, private land, tips, sites cleared for building, and plots of unoccupied land were the obvious choice. Within 12 hours of the sites being taken over, the balloons were in situ. When flying high over the city, this ingenious form of defence prevented enemy planes from diving low over the streets to make close-up attacks. During the Blitz of December 1940 all 72 balloons flew; 47 of them were damaged by shrapnel or enemy planes, but within 12 hours they had been repaired and were back to full strength. Maximum flying height of the barrage balloon was 6,000 ft. Only bad weather prevented the balloons from flying, and on occasions when the sirens sounded in unsuitable weather accidents happened. Sometimes the cables snapped setting the balloon free; on one frosty night 40 of them iced up and came down. The balloon being demonstrated in the photograph was sited on Crookesmoor recreation ground.

**Above:** Some Sheffielders sure to remember this spot - and what it was like before the Blitz of December 1941. It was around 7pm when the ominous wail of the air-raid sirens warned the city of the approach of enemy bombers. The 12th December was a Thursday, popular for an evening out, and the city's cinemas, dance halls and pubs had, as usual, tempted many into the city centre. When the sirens went most people made their way into the shelters. In the outlying suburbs those who had them went into their Anderson shelters; many went down to sit in the cellar or simply crowded together into the space below the staircase - the strongest part of the house. During the war Sheffield had a total of 130 air raid alerts, and during many of them no bombs fell. This one, however, was no false alarm. Before long people heard the distinctive sound of the German bombers and anti-aircraft guns. Flares were dropped to light up the city and soon the bombs began to fall. The raid lasted for nine hours, and many lost their lives. It turned out to be the first of a total of sixteen raids.

Above left: Angel Street was utterly devastated during the air raid of 12th December 1940; many buildings that had one minute been familiar city centre stores and shops were the next reduced to burning heaps of rubble and twisted metal. Like a scene from hell itself, every building left standing was on fire. H L Brown's jewellers, Dean and Dawson's booking agency, The Angel Hotel, Bortner's jewellers, Bell's bread shop, Crossley's drapers and many other city shops were wiped out. Cockaynes' smart department store had been a familiar landmark to Sheffielders for many years. The store was totally destroyed in the raid, and rebuilding on the site, in the foreground of this photograph, had just begun when the picture was taken. In the background Burton's building, on the right, is still standing though badly damaged. The Brightside and Carbrook Co-operative Society was also destroyed and a new building constructed. Buildings to the left of the photograph, at the top of Waingate, were demolished to make room for the new courthouse. The name of Cockaynes remained an icon in Sheffield until the store was taken over by Schofield's of Leeds in 1972. Ten years later the store closed its doors for the last time.

*Library staff cheerfully provided tea and a meal for those who had been unfortunate enough to have been bombed out during the Blitz that made them homeless just two weeks before Christmas in 1940. The library was not the only establishment that stepped in to help in the emergency. Within 24 hours of the raid an estimated 60,000 meals were supplied to homeless people. Many were fed in the blue and gold ballroom of the City Hall, where nourishing five-course meals were provided for the sum of tenpence. Large numbers of voluntary helpers turned out to lend a hand in the operation. The cooking and serving of the five-course meals was coordinated by experienced caterers, whose expertise ensured the smooth running of the massive undertaking. The City Hall British Restaurant had its important visitors: Home Secretary Mr Herbert Morrison not only came to see what was going on but sampled the food for himself, and their Majesties King George and Queen Elizabeth also dropped in on the restaurant. Did they also join the citizens of Sheffield for lunch? one wonders.*

**Left:** 'Many of the opportunities we have for replanning will not occur again,' states a planning document published in 1938 by the National Housing and Town Planning Council. Plans were afoot even then to clear crowded areas of housing. Only two years later the Luftwaffe provided the town planners with an opportunity to rebuild the city that was unlooked for and unwanted. A thousand private houses were totally demolished or were so badly damaged they had to be demolished. Two thousand homes were damaged though repairable. On the night of 12th December 1940 many stories of heroism were recorded of firefighters, ARP wardens and ambulance teams who laboured on hour after hour, putting out fires, clearing rubble, tending the wounded and trying to identify the dead. They rescued many from cellars and pulled whole families from the rubble of their demolished houses. It was around eleven hours before the all-clear sounded, and the citizens of Sheffield emerged from their shelters to find that a third of the city

centre had been wiped out in the raid. Around 30,000 incendiary bombs, 50 parachute mines and 1,200 high explosive bombs had been loosed on the city.

**Above:** A lone traffic policeman stands in the middle of Exchange Street, the only sign of life in scene that must have seemed like the end of the world. This section of road is clear, but after the raids it was impossible to travel through the city centre, as many main roads were blocked with enormous piles of smouldering rubble and burnt out buses and trams. During the nine hour raid that rocked the city of Sheffield to the core on the night of 12th December 1940, the rather elegant premises of the Brightside and Carbrook Co-operative Society had been described as 'a solid wall of flame'. It took another ten years before Sheffield once more had its well loved store; a one-storey building was erected as a stop-gap - strict building restrictions were still in place - and it took a few years more before other floors were added making it the popular department store we still have today.

**Above:** The building still stands, but all that was left of the Car & General Insurance Company's offices in Angel Street after the December raid was an empty shell. Fires spread to trams that were standing in the streets, and these burnt out trams were just two among a total of fourteen vehicles destroyed in the blitz. The war was a very difficult time for Sheffield's public transport in general and the tramway system in particular. Many of their staff enlisted in the services and women stepped in to replace them where possible. There were other dilemmas to face. Spare parts were like gold dust and were just as elusive. Yet petrol rationing, coupled with more workers commuting to factories, meant that more people than ever were using public transport. The blackout too caused many difficulties. 'Sparking' from the overhead tram wiring could be a problem. Headlamps were masked, allowing limited light to escape through a small slit, and drivers had to learn to 'feel' their way around the city streets, while inside the lights were so dim that the unfortunate conductresses scarcely knew whether they were being given a halfpenny or a shilling.

**Above right:** The morning after the night before…. On the morning of 13th December 1940 all that was left of the seven-storey Marples Hotel, on the left of the photograph, was a smoke-blackened pile of stones and rubble. There were a good number of guests in the hotel when the air raid alert sounded at 7pm on the evening

of the 12th. Staff and customers remained calm and kept their spirits up by having a sing-song in the lounge. The first German bombers were heard overhead within minutes of the siren sounding. As the bombs fell a number of windows on the ground floor were shattered and flying glass injured several people. They made their way to the cellars of the building, where soldiers treated their injuries with field dressings. That action might have saved a number of lives as soon afterwards the hotel took the full force of a direct hit from a high explosive bomb. Between 60 and 70 people were killed, but the true number of victims would never be known - only 14 of them could be identified. Around a thousand tons of rubble was moved in the rescue work and a few lucky survivors pulled from the wreckage.

**Above:** The night of 12-13th December 1940 was bright with stars when the alert was sounded at 7pm. Wave after wave of German bombers passed overhead, dropping their deadly load of incendiaries and high explosive bombs across Sheffield. Huge areas of the city were hit, and fed by fractured gas mains entire blocks of buildings quickly became a blazing inferno. Exhausted ARP wardens and firefighters - some of them from nearby towns - worked bravely on breathing air that was thick with smoke and fumes, while ash fell around them like snow. It often took days of hard work to make smouldering premises completely safe. The WVS mobile canteen (converted from a Rolls Royce) must have been a cheering sight to Sheffield's firemen and their auxiliaries, bringing them a cup of tea and a much needed break as they battled with coolness and courage hour after hour in unbelievable conditions to bring the fires under control. The drivers and volunteers manning the mobile canteens themselves often worked to the point of exhaustion to bring relief to the working parties around the city. Here WVS workers, ARP wardens and other workers in St Mary's Road take a quick break to pose for this photograph.

Wings for Victory Week - 28th May to 4th June 1943 - was a special time for all the citizens of Sheffield but particularly so for these children who were all pupils at Owler Lane School. The scheme was to encourage people to invest £4,000,000 in National Savings, which would provide 100 four-engined Lancaster bombers. The Lord Mayor was not above perching precariously on a table to demonstrate to the children that every time £100 was saved another plane was added to the board that declared optimistically 'The sky is the limit'.

Winston Churchill and his wife were in Sheffield to give the scheme the thumbs-up - or in case of 'Winnie' the two-fingered 'V for victory' sign. The public were bombarded with leaflets issued by Sheffield Savings Committee urging investment in savings stamps and certificates, National War Bonds, Defence Bonds and Post Office savings deposits. The week-long programme included boxing, a cricket match, demonstrations of unarmed combat and sea rescue, an RAF dance, and a grand parade of all the services including the Lincolnshire Regiment, mounted police, British Legion, Boys' Brigade and Girl Guides to name only a few, who marched to bands from Weston Park.

# Events & occasions

**Left:** The war was over, and the citizens of Sheffield were tired of bombs, gas masks, the blackout and all the other privations of wartime Britain. The entire community around Colwall Street went wild with joy when the news that everybody was waiting for was announced. Bunting was strung from house to house across the street, patriotic flags floated gently in the breeze, and 'Welcome Home' notices were painted to greet the returning troops. It was good to be alive, and along with the rest of Britain they found the energy to let their hair down and organise a knees-up after six long years of war. This scene was repeated in every street across the length and breadth of Great Britain. It was Britain's new Prime Minister, Clement Attlee, who brought the nation down from its euphoria with a bump. He warned the country that although Britain was once more at peace, there was no likelihood of prosperity for the country in the immediate future. Across the world countries were decimated by war, and there were worldwide food shortages. It would be several more years before people could stop using tinned dried eggs or shop for clothes without counting their coupons.

**Above:** There were no welcoming crowds to greet the Princess Royal when she visited Sheffield on 31st December 1940 - the visit was entirely unofficial, and the princess mingled unrecognised with workers and shoppers in the streets of the city. The Princess and her party received a few curious looks from passers-by, but few realised that this was a royal visit. The visit was so that the Princess Royal could see at first hand the damage that German bombers had done to Sheffield, and after making a tour of working class areas she called in to see the restaurant in the Town Hall where bombed-out families were provided with cheap meals. Her tour included a visit to Firvale House where the thousands of meals were prepared, and also the hospital where she chatted with some of the casualties of the raid. By the afternoon word of the royal visit had spread and crowds gathered to cheer and wave to the Princess. Younger readers might not realise that the Princess Royal was our Queen's aunt, Princess Victoria Alexandra Alice Mary, the only daughter of King George V. The title 'Princess Royal' is a comparatively recent title, instituted by King Edward VII.

**Left:** When King George VI and Queen Elizabeth visited Sheffield on 6th January 1941 it came as a complete surprise to everyone. Thousands would have turned out to cheer the royal couple had they known beforehand about the visit, but during the war strict security measures were needed to protect the nation's leaders. The King and Queen chatted with those who had suffered loss of their homes and loved ones during the bombing raids just a few short weeks before, and word soon spread that the royal couple were in town. 'Are we downhearted? No! Shall we win? Yes!' roared the crowd that quickly gathered. The King and Queen moved about the streets chatting with people, listening to the stories of their narrow escapes, their losses and the amazing heroism that characterised ordinary people in those dreadful days. One woman told the Queen of the wall she had built with her own hands to shield the entrance to her shelter; the wall saved her family's lives. Another told her of the furniture on which she had paid the final instalment the day before the raid that destroyed everything. The royal couple left marvelling at the amazing courage of the citizens of Sheffield.

**Above:** King George VI and Queen Elizabeth toured the ruins of bombed-out homes in a working class district when they visited Sheffield, the Queen even borrowing a pair of overshoes so that she could walk in the mud and debris. The royal couple heard many harrowing stories that day; they talked with an injured young man whose wife, child and mother-in-law had been killed in the air raid and his home destroyed. They talked to the widow whose husband had been one of ten wardens killed in an ARP post that had collapsed during the raid. They heard stories of the bravery of many unsung heroes, and Her Majesty's amazed comment was 'You still have a smile for us.' King George VI had been reluctant to take the throne; he was nervous and suffered from an embarrassing stammer (which he later overcame with medical aid and the support of his wife). 'I'm only a naval officer,' he confessed on the day he became king. 'It's the only thing I know about.' He had never seen a state paper. But he rose to the challenge and went on to take his place as perhaps Britain's most well loved monarch.

**Left:** What a welcome! A crowd of 20,000 people gathered in Town Hall Square to greet Winston Churchill on his visit to Sheffield on 8th November 1941, when he came to view the after effects of the Blitz and give encouragement to the people. Others lined the route that the Prime Minister's gleaming Daimler would take, craning their necks to catch a glimpse of the great man with his familiar fat cigar and his walking stick, returning his 'V for Victory' sign, hoarse with cheering and wild with excitement. Churchill spoke to the crowds in the Town Hall Square through loudspeakers, flaying the Nazis with his tongue, praising the citizens of the Steel City for their courage and endurance and cheering and encouraging them in the hardships that would undoubtedly lie ahead. Winston Churchill had seen war at first hand, fighting in Cuba, in India, and with Kitchener in Egypt, going on to become a war correspondent in the Boer War in South Africa. After that he went into Parliament, holding various offices. In May 1940 he became Prime Minister following Neville Chamberlain's resignation. Churchill went on to lead the country and inspire the British people throughout World War II.

**Below:** King George VI and Queen Elizabeth visited Sheffield on 25th September 1945 for the specific purpose of opening Ladybower Reservoir. The King and Queen had supported their subjects in every way possible during the war and had become well loved and popular everywhere. Vast crowds lined the route, determined to catch a glimpse of the royal visitors, and restraining the people's enthusiasm caused the police a real headache. It was the same story everywhere, with crowds pushing past the barriers and police to get as near to the cars as they could. Wounded soldiers and their nurses were among those who turned out to welcome the royal couple, and people crowded every window to obtain a vantage point. The 504 acre Ladybower Reservoir had been planned 46 years previously, and the King turned a small wheel to send water through the outlet valves. The reservoir had a total capacity of 6,300,000,000 gallons and would supply water to Nottingham, Leicester and Derby as well as Sheffield. Possibly the proudest man present was Frank Campbell. Seeing his Brownie box camera the King asked him if he would like a photograph; the royal couple posed especially for him. Where is that photograph today?

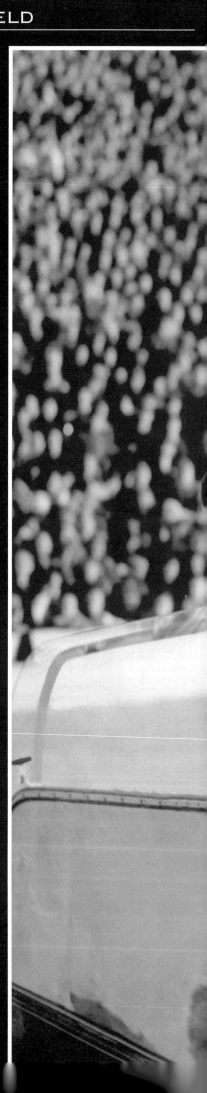

The Queen and the Duke visited the English Steel Corporation where they saw at first hand the city's traditional industry, and in the Siemens melting shop they watched as 90 tons of molten steel was tapped. The Queen asked perspiring workers how they endured the heat. The visit ended on a high note at a reception given in Sheffield Cutler's Hall, and possibly the largest crowd High Street has ever seen gathered to catch a glimpse of the royal couple. Naturally enough, the plate and cutlery at the reception was magnificent. The Queen and the Duke of Edinburgh each received a gift as a memento of their visit to Sheffield. The Queen was given a gold-chased penknife with blades of Sheffield stainless steel, while the Duke's gift was a yachting knife. Sheffield custom, of course, demands that a gift of knives must be paid for, and the Duke immediately coughed up the obligatory halfpenny. The Queen, however, was obviously strapped for cash but was saved from having to borrow from the Lord Mayor when she found a halfpenny lurking at the bottom of her little white bag. So ended a memorable visit during which the Queen and the Duke had endeared themselves to the people of Sheffield.

**Above:** Young patients from the City General Hospital and Firvale Infirmary were swathed in blankets as they and their nurses waited in Herries Road for three-quarters of an hour to see the Queen and Prince Philip on their two-day visit to Sheffield. The excited children were treated to more than a passing glimpse of the royal couple - their gleaming Rolls Royce slowed down to a crawl as it passed their party. It was a special day for many more sick and disabled Sheffielders who wanted to see the Queen. They were given VIP treatment - panes of glass from the front windows were completely removed to give patients from Middlewood Hospital an uninterrupted view of the royal visitors. Not everything passed off without a hitch. When the royal car approached the university to inaugurate the jubilee session the royal standard was found to be too high to pass beneath the ceremonial entrance. After that all went well, and the Queen said she had very much enjoyed the occasion. 'Right royal weather' greeted the Queen and the Duke on their visit, however - 50 minutes before they arrived to take lunch at the Town Hall the sun broke through over Sheffield for the first time in days.

Office workers perched precariously on five-storey windowsills to get a better view of the royal party when the Queen and the Duke of Edinburgh visit Sheffield in October 1954. Schoolchildren were given a holiday, and one of the high notes of the visit was a rally at the Sheffield Wednesday ground at Hillsborough, where 3,000 children lined up on the pitch forming the words 'Welcome to Sheffield'. Sheffielders all wanted to see the Queen, and they were prepared to wait for two hours or more as long as they could get a good view along the route. One enterprising elderly lady solved her own problem by taking a chair on to the roundabout opposite the police station. Crowds in the Wicker were four deep as they waved and cheered their welcome. The Queen and the Duke were met at the Town Hall by the Lord Mayor, Ald J H Bingham. At luncheon in the banqueting room a dainty sugar casket topped with a crown and 'E II R' was placed in front of Her Majesty. The casket contained sweetmeats. Disappointingly, the Queen declined to eat any of it - perhaps, like hundreds of women country wide - she was watching her figure.

# Bird's eye view

This aerial view of Sheffield was captured in 1955. The wedge-shaped building in the centre of the photograph is the premises of George Kennings Motor Group situated between Paternoster Row and Shoreham Street. Above and slightly to the left, distinguished by its long rooftops, is the Shoreham Street tram sheds and the adjoining bus sheds. The Shoreham Street depot was opened in February 1911, and was large enough to take a total of 114 tramcars. For the interest of lovers of trivia, at the time this photograph was taken Sheffield had 13 tram services. Unfortunately the routes were not numbered, though tickets displayed an unofficial route designation. Sheffield was noted for its low fares - the maximum fare in the early 1950s was threepence.

The site across the road from George Kennings was eventually occupied by a college annexe and by the six-storey British Rail offices, which is still in use. The many buildings and railway lines make the nearby station easy to spot. At the bottom centre of the photograph Pond street leads diagonally off towards the bus station past what could be the first phase of Pond Street College.

Much of the area covered by this 1955 photograph is very different today. Many of the old buildings are no longer there and a network of new highways now sweeps through and around Sheffield's city centre. Some of the old buildings, however, fortunately survive, and the Town Hall is at the centre of the photograph. The familiar 'egg box' extension was added in the 1970s. Over the years Sheffield has had at least four Town Halls; back in 1637 a survey makes reference to a 'Towne Halle' which was built over eleven shops. The nearby St Paul's Church was demolished in the late 1930s and St Paul's Gardens was designed and planted on the site. The official name, however, was ignored and Sheffielders insisted on calling them the Peace Gardens. After 50 years the City Council gave in and made this the official name. Beyond the roundabout at the top of Fargate is the City Hall, easily distin-guished by its elegant semicircular extension at the rear. The building saw much controversy over the years, particu-larly about the pair of Assyrian lions that stood on the stage in the auditorium. Some loved them, some hated them, but at least nobody ignored them!

**Below:** Appearing from this height rather like children's Lego bricks, the Broomhall housing scheme is bounded by the Hanover Way inner city ring road and Eccleshall Road in the top right hand corner of this aerial view, taken in 1970. The name of Ward's Brewery is a household word in the city of Sheffield, and almost thirty years after this photograph was taken the brewery to the right of Eccleshall Road is still producing good beer. Cemetery Road is the long straight road on the right hand side of the photograph, and many Sheffielders will recognise the extensive premises of the Sheffield Twist Drill Co on Cemetery Road even from above. To their left is James Neill's hacksaw blades and tools business, while to the right is the Lansdowne Flats development, and on the opposite side of the road readers might be able to pick out Cemetery Road Baptist Church, which has been a well-known landmark in the city for many years. Washington Road leads off to the right. Davy's Computers, at the very top of the picture, has gone and a branch of Safeway now serves the community's shopping needs.

**Above:** The M1 motorway bisects this historic photograph taken in 1967 that captures the construction of Junction 34 at Tinsley and linkup of the motorway with Leeds. Motorways were introduced in response to the growing traffic problems - in the early 1960s one in seven people owned a car, and accidents, pollution and noise prompted drastic plans to help traffic to move faster and avoid town centre bottlenecks. In 1959 the first 75 miles of the M1 motorway were opened, and over the next 25 years 750 miles of motorway were built. The twin cooling towers of the Blackburn Meadows Power Station still provide a landmark that is known to the thousands of motorists that use theM1 motorway every day. The cooling towers further to the right, however, have since been demolished. The gas holders that form a vital part of the Wincobank Gas Works are still there. The extensive premises of Hadfields East Hecla Steel Works can be seen to the left of the photograph; the men fought hard to save their jobs and the company, but by the mid 1980s Hadfields had been demolished. Today the gigantic Meadowhall shopping complex, with a higher turnover than London's Oxford Street, occupies the site.

*The Moor draws the eye from the bottom right hand corner of the photograph along its unmistakable unbroken length towards The Town Hall and the Peace Gardens at the top centre. The white building to the right of the Town Hall is the Central Library and Graves Art Gallery situated almost alongside Arundel Gate. Next door to the library but not clearly seen in this photograph is the Lyceum Theatre which began entertaining Sheffield theatregoers more than 100 years ago. It was then called the City Theatre, replacing Alexander Stacey's Circus, an earlier wooden building that was destroyed by fire in 1893. The Lyceum eventually closed, but was given a new lease of life in recent years, reopening in 1990. The theatre's grand staircase and pleasant bar are features that linger in the memory of most visitors. Sheffield's famous Crucible Theatre stands nearby. Near the library the distinctive and unusual shape of the Register Office reminds us of the reason the citizens of Sheffield dubbed it 'The Wedding Cake'. The circular building replaced the older premises in Surrey Street. The structure further down the Moor which appears wedge-shaped from this viewpoint is the offices of Yorkshire Television.*

The city of Sheffield lies far below us like a 3D map in this eagle's eye view, and three roads from the outlying areas lead like arteries to the heart of the city at the top right of the photograph. The headquarters of the Manpower Services Commission can be seen near the ring road, towards the bottom right of the picture. The 'dog leg' of Arundel Gate passes the Register Office, the Town Hall's 'egg box' extensions, the Novotel, the Central Library and the Crucible Theatre. Recognisable from its distinctive layered roof, the Crucible has gained fame from its status as a venue for the World Snooker Championships. The modern circular layout of the building and its tiered rows of seats lends itself to certain types of drama and sport.

The Town Hall is easily picked out. Further to the left and less easy to spot, is the City Hall in Barker's Pool. Barker's Pool itself dates back around 500 years, when a Mr Barker built a reservoir to conserve spring water. The pool was removed at the end of the 18th Century, but the name lived on. Barker's Pool was home to two well known theatres, the Albert Hall and the Gaumont.

# On the move

**Left:** A rather nice Vauxhall 10, with a Morris 8 close behind, are in the foreground of this photograph, taken in the Moor in July 1939. The coats and hats of the ladies bear silent testimony to what was evidently a typical English summer's day. The tram is bound for Angel Street in the city centre. At this time war was only on the horizon and the horrors that changed the appearance of this long straight thoroughfare for all time. The enormous Manpower Services Commission building, rising from the end of the Moor like an ancient Aztec pyramid, has added its own flavour to the city redevelopments. Much of the Moor has today become a very pleasant pedestrianised market area, with central covered stands that shelter stall-holders from the worst of the British weather. From time to time a children's funfair is set up there, to the delight of all the kiddies.

**Below:** Pond Street bus and tram station has been serving the people of Sheffield for many years. The first motor bus service was established in Sheffield in 1913 and ran in conjunction with the horse tram which had for many years been the city's usual form of public transport. The first tram line, between Lady's Bridge and Attercliffe, was opened on 6th October 1873. A journey on those early trams was hardly a luxury ride, they had uncomfortable wooden slat seats, straw was laid on the floor, and a couple of oil lamps gave out what light they could. Sheffield's earliest form of station for public transport was a 'commodious inn', which was built in the late 1780s by a group of businessmen in response to increasing demands on the coach services The £4,000 cost was raised by 50 subscribers who each gave £100 and in turn received an equal share of profits and rents. The result was the Tontine, the city's largest coaching inn. The express service between London, Sheffield and Leeds, carried only four passengers inside, and left the Tontine at 11am every day, arriving in London at 1pm the following day.

*Davy's Cafe is immediately to the left of this 1953 photograph, which looks towards Waingate. The number of private cars had increased by the 1950s, but the photograph shows that there is still a respectable number of buses and trams about. A tram bound for Sheffield Lane Top via Pitsmoor passes, with a Handsworth tram behind. The shells of bombed-out buildings can still be seen on the horizon, and though the speed with which Sheffield got down to rebuilding after the war was amazing, there still remained much to be done. The date was 7th November, obviously a chilly day, and it is interesting to note that head coverings of one kind and another were still very much in vogue in the early 1950s. Many of the ladies here are wearing headscarves, which though not regarded as high fashion today were a very sensible way to keep warm and dry. They were in good company - her Majesty the Queen, who came to the throne that year, was a very keen wearer of headscarves. The men in the photograph are sporting flat caps. Interestingly the motor cycle rider is not wearing a crash helmet.*

It was 1955, and the bus station in Pond Street was just a year away from its first face lift. The layout would stay essentially the same while the bus shelters themselves were closed in for the comfort of passengers. Escalators and bridges would be added to provide links with nearby shops. Further developments in the 1990s gave the bus station a second reshuffle and the neat and simple new arrangements were a great improvement - people new to the city and the bus routes found it much easier to find their way around. The railway station, which can just be picked out in the background of this photograph, was itself very tastefully modernised, and with an eye to conservation the original frontage was retained. Brownie points to the architect. The station was linked to the bus station by a convenient covered walkway.

**Below:** Tram number 134 (which was in service between 1929 and 1958) negotiates Town Hall Square on its way to Millhouses in 1949, and the busy scene also includes a motor bus. Sheffield never had trolley buses, though it was discussed back in 1908, and coincidentally the Millhouses route was one of those put forward for a trial. However, the scheme was not pursued and the 'trackless' never appeared in Sheffield. Wilson Peck was a high-class music shop well known to all Sheffield's music lovers who might have bought a piano or a radiogram there, and almost certainly at some time a record. Wilson Peck's prominent advert for His Master's Voice records is one of the 20th Century's most well known trade-marks. The small dog in HMV's well-known ad was Nipper, whose master, the English painter Francis Barraud borrowed a gramophone with a large horn so that he could paint his dog alongside it. The Gramophone Company ended up buying the picture and adopted it as their trademark. The company later became RCA Victor and continued to use Nipper, who has ended up as possibly the most famous dog in the world. A firm of jewellers now occupies the same premises.

Readers will have heard the old saying that you wait half an hour for a bus and then along come five all at once. The same saying obviously applied to trams, and a tram bound for Crookes heads this view of five that are within the range of the camera lens in Sheffield High Street in 1953. Despite the volume of traffic that includes both public transport and private cars, pedestrians still risk life and limb as they cross the road. During World War II no new cars were manufactured and petrol was strictly rationed, and after the war Britain had a shortage of steel. There was an enormous demand for public transport, and whether you were going to the cinema or commuting to work you usually travelled by bus. By the end of the decade, however, the situation was beginning to change, and in 1953, the year this photograph was taken, petrol rationing was at last brought to an end. Wives as well as husbands were going out to work, and the average family had more money than ever before. Once more there was a demand for cheap small cars such as the Morris Minor and the Austin A40.

**Above:** Sheffield's tram and bus services were hard hit during the blitz of December 1940, and six employees were killed and fourteen others injured whilst on duty. Large sections of tram track and overhead wiring were destroyed and a number of cars were burnt out in the bombing raids. Tram services were temporarily suspended until repairs could be made to the track and wiring. In 1942 a number of replacement trams were purchased from Bradford Corporation. Among them was this ex Bradford Corporation tram whose upper deck was removed when it was turned into a works car. The long-lived vehicle, as can be seen in this photograph, was still in service in Abbey Lane in July 1957. The same tram can be seen today at Crich Tramway Museum in Derbyshire, where amazingly it is still in use as a works tram. Lovers of trivia might like to know that Bradford's tramlines were 4ft gauge while Sheffield's were 4ft 8 1/2ins. When the trams were transferred to Sheffield the difference in wheel width was overcome by mounting the bodies on Sheffield trucks (chassis). Bradford trams had open-ended top decks; when Sheffield acquired them the upper decks were enclosed after the preferred Sheffield style.

*Pond Street Bus Station in the 1940s was a very different place from the modern building that eventually emerged over the following decades. These original open sided shelters gave little protection from the elements in those early days, and waiting in a queue for a bus was a very chilly experience. Fortunately there were plenty of buses and trams - the city had an excellent public transport service, so one would assume that travellers did not have very long to wait. The bus station was at that time overlooked by Thomas Rawson's Brewery and other old shops and houses, some of which can be seen on the left of the picture; they were later demolished to make way for the College of Technology which later became the Polytechnic and was eventually given university status. In 1956 the first covered bus station was built, a real convenience that was much appreciated by commuters and by holidaymakers bound for the seaside. In the background the GPO can be picked out against the skyline; the flat-roofed sorting office lies behind a group of buses below. Many travellers have enjoyed the odd pint at the Penny Black Pub; it is not clear whether the pub was there when this photograph was taken.*

**Left:** Sheffield's tramway was determined to go out in style, and during the last week of tram services an illuminated tramcar toured the streets in the black and yellow livery that was used in 1760 for the stage coach service between Sheffield and London. Readers who were among the crowds that gathered on the 8th October 1960, the last day of Sheffield trams, will remember it as much for the torrential downpour as for the nostalgia of the occasion. The final procession of 15 tramcars left Tenter Street Depot at 6pm, and heedless of the downpour people lined the route to cheer and wave as the trams passed. At the rear of the procession was Tram No 510; in the floodlit Town Hall Square a wreath was placed on her front bumper to the strains of 'Auld Lang Syne' played by the Transport Band, and thousands joined in the singing. A fitting end to the old tramway. The photograph shows people placing coins on the track; the resulting bent coins made rather nice souvenirs. Sheffield was the last industrial city in England with a tram service - and the intro-duction of the South Yorkshire Supertram has of course brought the story full circle.

**Above:** The clock on the distinctive tower of Victoria Station informs travellers that the time is 12.16. The station was still well used in July 1967, as can be seen from the number of cars parked on the station forecourt. Only three years on, however, the well loved old station that had been carrying passengers on the Woodhead route since 1851 was to close. It was later demolished and today the site remains empty, though the Victoria Hotel is still open. A rumour circulates that the line is scheduled for revival..only time will tell. The railway came to Sheffield in 1838. Off picture to the left, the railway, which was electrified in the early 1950s, ran over the Wicker arches. Passengers could reach the station by way of steps or by lift from the Wicker. Victoria Station was traditionally the home of memorial plaques which bore a tribute to the British Rail employees who gave their lives in the Great War. When the station was demolished the plaques were removed and were re-sited below the Wicker arches.

**Above:** Apart, of course, for the tram on the Woodseats Road, Millhouses route, this scene at the Firth Park Road and Owler Lane junction remains virtually unchanged since it was captured on camera in April 1960. Perhaps the date gives us a clue to the reason the photograph was taken, as Sheffield's trams had only another six months to go before the service was discontinued. Discontinued, that is, until 1992, when the state of the art Supertram service was introduced to the city. The shops along this stretch of road are still there, though today a number of them bear different names and several others are takeaway food shops. Sheffield established its very first form of public transport between towns as long ago as 1760, when Samuel Glanville started up a coach service from Leeds to London via Sheffield. He described it as a 'Flying Machine', though as many of the roads were at that time still stony and full of holes it could not have flown very fast. The journey from Leeds in fact took three days and six hours to reach London, with overnight stops at Nottingham and Northampton.

# Shopping spree

The date of this photograph is 22nd May 1937, which gives us a clue to the reason for the flags, bunting and garlands that decorate the buildings in Haymarket. The Coronation of King George VI had taken place a week or so previously on 12th May, and the citizens of Sheffield, never slow to recognise the opportunity to party, had really gone to town for the occasion. The new king had never been destined for the throne, he was a shy family man who had the role of the sovereign thrust upon him when his brother King Edward VIII abdicated in order to marry American divorcee Wallis Simpson. King George dutifully took up the reins, encouraged by his beautiful queen, and went on to shepherd his country through the Second World War and become one of the most popular sovereigns in history. The most noticeable thing about the photograph is the sheer volume of public transport, and it is interesting to note that trams far outnumber the motor buses in Haymarket. Few ordinary working people at that time owned a motor car, which was still very much regarded as being a middle class symbol, and people depended heavily on public transport.

**Above:** A little piece of history began with this sweet shop in Norfolk Street, Sheffield. It was back in 1911 that Joseph William Thornton moved his family into the rooms above and opened his little shop, giving the 'Chocolate Kabin' the distinctive spelling that was to make it famous. His aim was to make it 'the nicest sweet shop in town'. He certainly succeeded, and by 1939 the Thorntons company had 25 shops in the Midlands and around Yorkshire. In the late 1990s Thorntons coined the memorable advertising slogan 'Chocolate heaven since 1911'; after nearly 90 years in production their goodies are still a delight to chocoholics everywhere. Pictured here in December 1940 right after the Blitz that destroyed a large part of the city centre, we can see that Thorntons had a miraculous escape. Other Thornton shops were not so lucky; eight of them were destroyed in Nazi bombing raids, including the branches in Fitzalan Square and Rockingham Street, Sheffield.

**Right:** The Castle House Number One Co-op had its grand opening in 1950, and long queues had formed in Angel Street long before the doors opened for the first time. The original building had been destroyed in World War II. To celebrate Opening Day potential customers and staff alike posed in the shoe department for this photograph. Instead of the shelves of shoes on display that we are used to today, back in 1950 most of the shoes were tucked away in boxes, as in this picture where you can see them stacked up at the back of the shop. Some readers will remember the days when you sat down in a shoe shop and told an attentive staff member exactly what kind of footwear you were looking for. 'I need a pair of brown shoes with flat heels, please; something comfortable - slip-ons rather than lace-ups.' Customers might have had to wait a while longer in the shop, but at least they had the benefit of personal attention from the staff. See it, try it and buy it has become the norm in these days when staffing levels have been trimmed to cut costs, and we have become a self serve society.

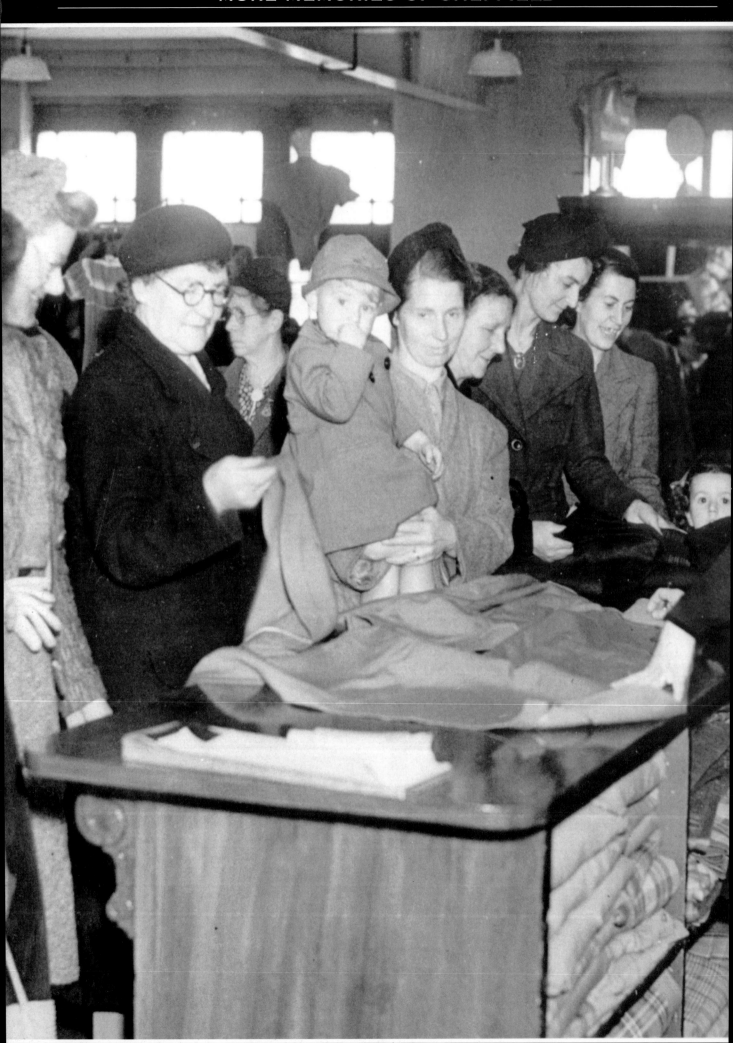

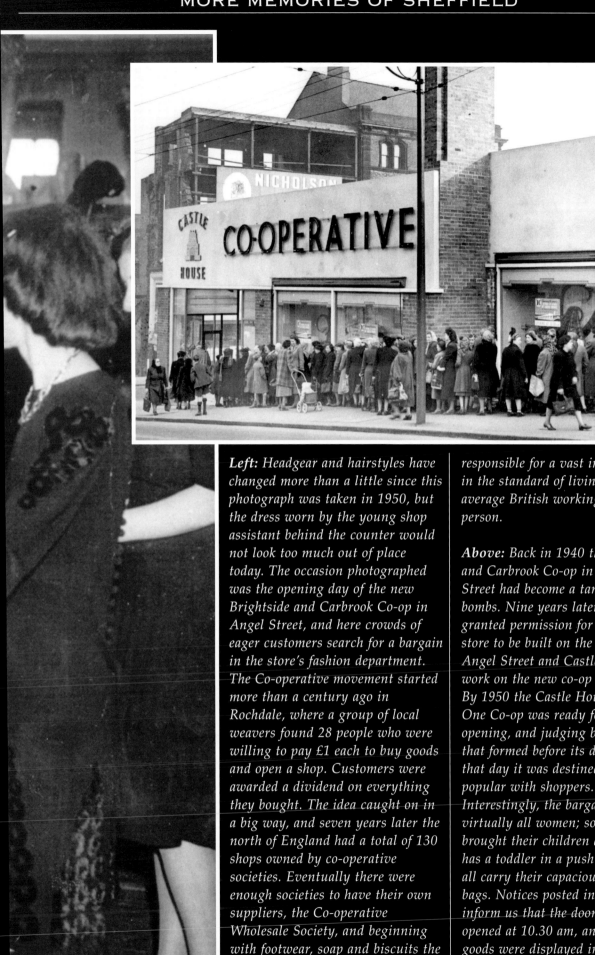

**Left:** Headgear and hairstyles have changed more than a little since this photograph was taken in 1950, but the dress worn by the young shop assistant behind the counter would not look too much out of place today. The occasion photographed was the opening day of the new Brightside and Carbrook Co-op in Angel Street, and here crowds of eager customers search for a bargain in the store's fashion department. The Co-operative movement started more than a century ago in Rochdale, where a group of local weavers found 28 people who were willing to pay £1 each to buy goods and open a shop. Customers were awarded a dividend on everything they bought. The idea caught on in a big way, and seven years later the north of England had a total of 130 shops owned by co-operative societies. Eventually there were enough societies to have their own suppliers, the Co-operative Wholesale Society, and beginning with footwear, soap and biscuits the CWS began to manufacture its own goods, provide insurance and arrange affordable funerals. During the earlier years of the 20th Century the Co-op movement was responsible for a vast improvement in the standard of living of the average British working class person.

**Above:** Back in 1940 the Brightside and Carbrook Co-op in Exchange Street had become a target for Nazi bombs. Nine years later the Council granted permission for a one-storey store to be built on the corner of Angel Street and Castle Street, and work on the new co-op was begun. By 1950 the Castle House Number One Co-op was ready for its grand opening, and judging by the queue that formed before its doors opened that day it was destined to be popular with shoppers. Interestingly, the bargain seekers are virtually all women; some have brought their children along, one has a toddler in a push chair - but all carry their capacious shopping bags. Notices posted in the windows inform us that the doors were to be opened at 10.30 am, and bargain goods were displayed in all the windows. Note the buildings around the corner in Castle Street, which still show signs of bomb damage and are in the process of reconstruction.

**Right:** We have grown so used to pedestrianised areas in the major shopping streets of Sheffield that it seems strange to look back at Fargate with traffic. This view of Fargate was taken in 1954, 17 years before traffic was banned. Town Hall Square has lived through a multitude of changes over the years. In 1888 the Jubilee Monolith, a striking 390ft high memorial surrounded by ornate gas lamps, was erected to mark Queen Victoria's Golden Jubilee, and Fargate was widened in the same year to take the increase in traffic. The Monolith was removed in 1904 and taken to Endcliffe Park. The Yorkshire Penny Bank, to the right of the photograph, was built for the Bank in 1888-89; the right hand side of the building was occupied by the Albany, a temperance hotel reached by an entrance in Surrey Street. In 1958 the hotel closed and the building's use changed to offices. The pleasant dormer windows and chimneys that had graced the roof line of the building for many years were removed and a modern addition was built that no doubt provided office workers with more light but was totally out of keeping with the rest of the building.

**Below:** The Moor was fighting its way back into existence by 1952; it had been all but obliterated by enemy bombs and on the night of the worst raid much of the road was a sea of flames. Deacons Bank, Atkinson's Stores and many other shops, offices, houses and pubs were destroyed. Ironically the Peace Monument survived, and can be seen on the left of this picture beyond Woolworths, which is in the same place today. Burtons menswear shop further along is now the premises of Vision Express. The scars of war are still plain to see on Phillips' Furnishing Stores Ltd, and their large hoarding informs passers by that 'All our furniture carries a lifetime's guarantee'.

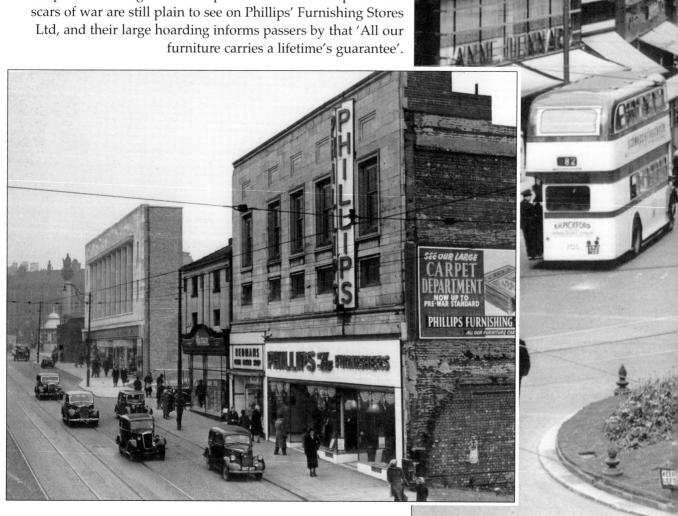

*A marriage of different architectural styles brought the Wilson Peck building and Cinema House together in an uneasy union which Sheffielders through the years grew used to having around. Wilson Peck had been 'making music' for Sheffield since long before the popularity of television, but the company kept well in step with public demand.Cinema House was designed along grand lines, and the building's double staircase in green and white marble was one of its familiar features. Opened on 6th May 1913, the cinema's opening was 'Theodora' and 'Construction of the panama Canal', silent movies, of course. In 1914 they gave exclusive displays of Edison's Kinetophone Synchronised Sound, but Cinema House was actually one of the last of Sheffield's cinemas to convert to sound. The first 'talkie', shown on 24th February 1930, was 'Climbing the Golden Stair', a musical filmed in early Technicolor. Back in 1914 you would have paid 1/- to see a varied programme in a good seat at Cinema House (five pence in today's currency, which near the beginning of the 21st Century seems cheap but was fairly steep back then). The last film was shown on 12th August 1961, and the building was then demolished for redevelopment.*

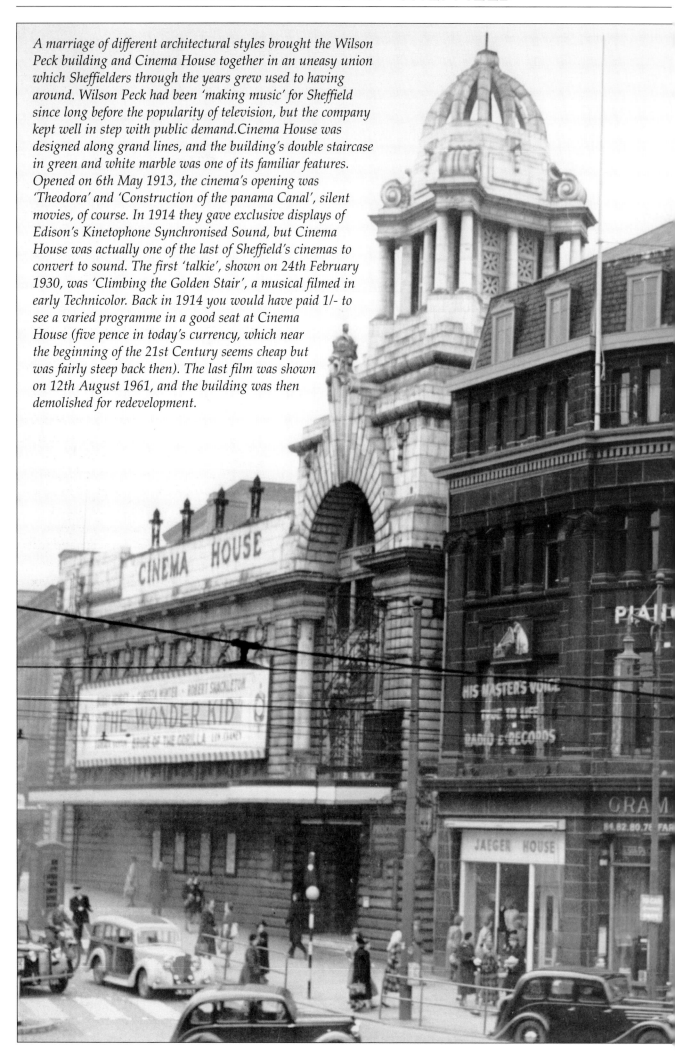

**Below:** This view of Fargate in 1957 still included tramlines. Though Sheffield's trams were slowly being superseded by motor buses, tram services went on serving the city throughout the 1950s, and were finally discontinued at the end of the decade. Looking from Town Hall Square down Fargate, the former offices of the Telegraph & Star - now Bradford & Bingley Building Society - are in the centre of the photograph. Its distinctive tower and clock have been a familiar High Street landmark since it was built to replace older properties demolished in 1913-14. In 1957 the flower beds on the Town Hall Square roundabout continued to brighten up the city centre. The Sir Stuart and Lady Goodwin Fountain was presented to the city in 1961 and quickly established itself as a well loved Sheffield landmark. Forty-six feet in diameter, the fountain jetted water towards a stainless steel band in the centre, a symbol of the development in Sheffield of stainless steel in 1913. Today Fargate is a pedestrian shopping precinct, and the lack of traffic makes browsing among the city's many fascinating shops a much more pleasant experience.

**Bottom:** This atmospheric view of Fitzalan Square was captured on camera in 1952. The lovely old building with the dome was Barclays Bank, now of course demolished. The News Theatre adjoining the bank has a long and interesting history. The cinema was opened as the Electra Palace in February 1911, carrying on the well established tradition of entertainment on that site - the position was previously occupied by Wonderland, an amusement palace that held displays of animated pictures. The 900-seat Electra was the first cinema to establish continuous shows, inviting the public to 'come when you please, leave when you please'. It must have been a very pleasant place to spend an afternoon or

evening, positioned in front of the screen was a tasteful arrangement of plants, roses and moss and people were served with light refreshments as they sat in their seats. The Electra boasted an entire change of pictures every Monday and Thursday, and seats in the balcony - the best in the house - would have only set you back one shilling. The site on the right of the photograph was once occupied by the ill-fated Marples Hotel, which was destroyed with great loss of life by enemy bombs in 1940.

**Left:** The 'Rag 'n Tag' was always a popular place for Sheffielders to pick up a bargain, and many of the old shops seen here - Tom Marsh's, Granelli's, Binghams, Coates' flowers and greengrocers shop and Ogley's pet and aquarium stores - were an accepted part of life, as familiar to Sheffielders as the nose on their own faces. On this wet day in 1963, however, the market wore a rather forlorn and deserted air - the shops are obviously closed. Enormous changes have been made in the area over the years. The Broad Street public loos on the left of the photograph were not the only well known buildings to disappear in Sheffield's improvement and modernisation schemes. The older properties in the background were also demolished in the road building scheme that gave Park Square to the city. Nearby Commercial Street is today part of the Supertram route, and the state of the art tram passes across the Park Square development. The old Sheaf Market pictured here eventually disappeared and was replaced by an indoor Sheaf Market, which was replaced by yet another one.... The Sheaf Market has now closed its doors on the shoppers of Sheffield - but is it for the last time? Watch this space!

**Above:** Shoppers and outdoor displays bring the old Sheaf Market to life and make the popularity of the old open air market evident. Pet baskets and other goods displayed on the outer walls of Ogley's walk-round 'super pet store' made the shop attractive to punters, and the open air fruit vegetable stall did the same for H Coates' flower shop. The date is 1964, and readers will be able to see that Sheffield's Park Hill Flats are already under construction on the skyline. The extensive Park Hill and Hyde Park developments were completed within two years. The new flats, some of them 17 storeys high, were Sheffield's answer to the city's severe housing shortage, providing homes for around 3,000 residents. But pride in the new project was short-lived and the area eventually became run-down. The high-rise flats were all demolished; some of the low-rise blocks were modernised and a number of them were used as a Games Village during the 1991 World Student Games. It was in 1964, the year of this photograph, that the rather handsome old Corn Exchange Building not too far away in Sheaf Street was demolished in the city's enormous road building scheme.

**Above:** Foster's sweets and tobacco shop right next to the bottom entrance to the Sheaf Market in Commercial Street. How many Sheffielders passed under that large sign above the entrance over the years? The photograph looks towards Haymarket and Waingate, and in the centre background the Woolworths building dominates the skyline. The Woolworths building was constructed on the site of the old Norfolk Market Hall. Sheffield has a long tradition of excellent markets, and the Norfolk Market was built in 1851 at a cost of around £40,000. The Penny Bazaar was a popular calling place for Sheffield's canny shoppers - much as the original Marks and Spencers, the stall sold nothing that cost more than a penny. To trace the history of the site even further back, the Norfolk Market Hall replaced the ancient Tontine coaching inn. When the railway reached Sheffield in 1838 the death knell sounded for coaching, and the Duke of Norfolk purchased the Tontine so that he could demolish it for his new market. Just out of sight in this 1970 photograph is the new Castle Market, opened in 1962.

**Right:** This fascinating photograph gives us a glimpse across the Sheaf Market at the clearance and levelling operations that prepared the way for the vast Park Square roundabout and the A61 development that provided a link with the M1 motorway. Full of character and tradition, these images of the Sheaf Market and its shops and stalls provide the citizens of Sheffield with that little glimpse into their past that most people need. Readers who harbour a few nostalgic thoughts of the Sheaf Market might remember, for example, the market's 'guess your weight' man. After estimating how much you weighed he would then seat you in a hanging chair to check his guess against the scales. Remember, too, the man who sold china; he would take a handful of plates from his basket and juggle with them, throwing them in the air and catching them again, all the time accompanying the feat with his steady sales patter. Nobody remembers him ever dropping any of them!

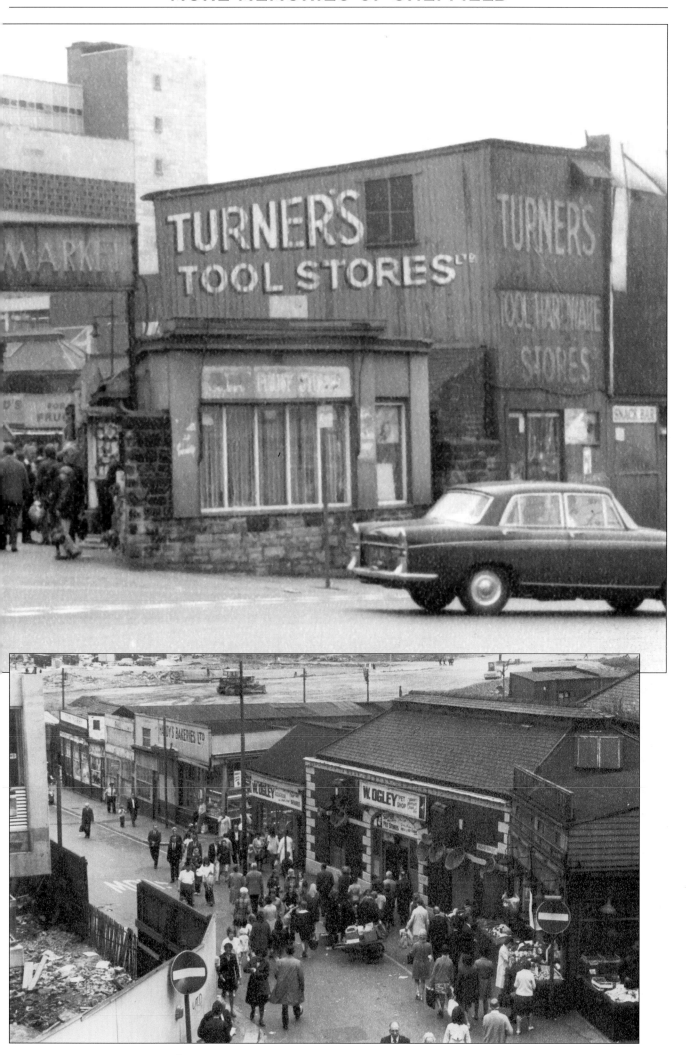

The year is 1961; the trams disappeared from the streets of Sheffield the previous year, but their legacy of tramlines would be around for some time to come. Renovation and construction work is still going on around the city, and the store to the left of Haymarket in the photograph wears a framework of scaffolding that is boarded off from the public thoroughfare. Built on the site previously occupied by the old Norfolk Market Hall, the new store later opened as Woolworths. Further along is Burtons (their large store in High Street was badly damaged during World War II), and Liptons. In the central background is the General Post Office in Fitzalan Square, and to the right of the GPO a tower crane reaches skywards as another of Sheffield's new buildings is brought into being. On the right of the picture is Davy's Mikado Cafe and Weaver to Wearer menswear shop. The blinds above the windows of the shop on the far right remind us that this is Davy's food store, whose large premises continue around the corner. Davy's was a hugely popular place to shop, and their mouthwatering pies, cornish pasties and tomato sausages were legendary.

# At work

**Below:** The police information room at Endcliffe Grange in 1933 was a very different place from today's equivalent. The staff in this photograph appear to total one police officer and a telephone operator, and their operations are obviously coordinated by means of a wall map and an illuminated display. Crime figures were far lower, however, and in 1937 the Sheffield City Police had a small fleet of 15 motor vehicles. During that particular year the Sheffield force had a total of four instances of 'taking away vehicles without the owner's consent'. Today the number of cars stolen might be nearer four a minute! There were far fewer private cars on the road, and Sheffield only had seven sets of traffic lights. The developments that would take place before the end of the century could never have been visualised by the staff in this obviously chilly information room (note the telephonist's warm boots). In the early 1970s the county boundaries changed, bringing about one of the great transformations; Sheffield City Police amalgamated with Doncaster, Rotherham and Barnsley to become South Yorkshire Constabulary. Today's police control rooms have an enormous staff, banks of networked computers, a police helicopter, and radio links with every car.

**Right:** The driver and conductor of tram number 522 pose with their vehicle in Abbeydale Road in 1960. Was this a special occasion - a birthday perhaps, or the retirement of one of the team? Or did they simply think that having a souvenir photograph taken was a jolly good idea? We shall never know, but nevertheless it is interesting to speculate. According to its destination blind the Tram is bound for Vulcan Road. The tram has the well-known Roberts body made by Charles Robert in Wakefield. An identical vehicle is at present running at Beamish folk museum after being parked - or perhaps the word should be preserved - for a time at Oxenhope railway station, near Keighley. Back in the days of the horse buses, a service once ran from the Royal Hotel in Abbeydale Road to Carterknowle Road bottom. Routes were being established across the city, and each had its own operator. On the Abbeydale Road route passengers were charged a penny to travel the one-mile journey. Horse trams, introduced to Sheffield in 1886, proved to be more efficient than the old horse buses which eventually went out of business.

The work of the police involves a wide variety of duties, and establishing friendly links with the general public is far from being the least important. The traffic warden chatting with the passer by and her grandchild in Exchange Street demonstrates the point. By 1968 the number of private cars on the road was still increasing, and shepherding children safely across the road was an important part of police work. In 1968, the date of these fascinating images, South Yorkshire Constabulary was yet to be formed, and school crossing patrols, known affectionately to all as 'Lollipop men' (or ladies!) and traffic wardens

were two divisions of Sheffield City Police.

A less pleasant side of police work demands that officers attend the scene of accidents. The date given for the accident pictured is 1968, though its precise location is not known. We can only hope that these trucks were the only casualties.

The engine is a Class 40 made by English Electric at Loughborough, while the damaged guard's van is a standard 20 ton British Rail brake van. The wagon on the left in front of the engine is a steel standard 16 ton mineral wagon. To you and me, a coal truck.

# From tea set to jet set – the company that forges ahead

What is the connection between a set of hand-forged silver cutlery and a collection of high quality components for the aircraft industry?

Sounds like one of those enigmatic pub quiz questions, doesn't it? But this is no trick question; the answer is C W Fletcher & Sons Ltd of Sheffield. Established more than a hundred years ago, Fletchers of Sheffield has developed over the intervening years into a company with a foot firmly planted in both industries.

The city of Sheffield has for hundreds of years been connected with steel making and engineering, together with the lighter trades of metal tableware and cutting tools. During the later years of the last century a keen young apprentice, Charles William Fletcher, served his time in Sheffield's traditional industry and emerged as an amazingly talented silversmith and silver hand forger.

**Right:** *C.W Fletcher and family*
**Below:** *Works outing to Castleton around 1909.*

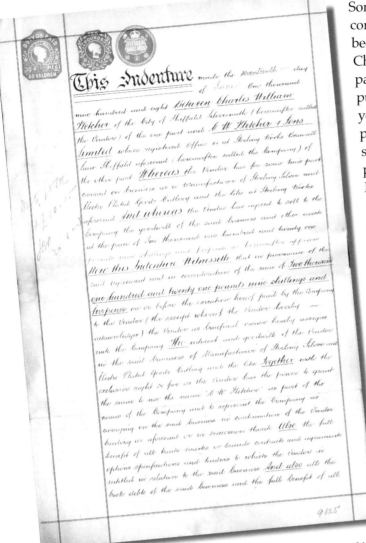

Some months previously Charles Fletcher had committed himself to buying the factory, and had been paying monthly sums towards that end. On Christmas Eve 1903 he signed over the final payment - and the factory was his. The full purchase price was £707.10s, which a hundred years on appears to be quite a small price for the purchase of a factory, but was at that time a sizeable sum of money that had to be found and paid little by little. Charles Fletcher's wife Hannah and their young family may not have enjoyed many presents that particular year, but all the same it must have been a memorable Christmas for the entire family. They were committed; the dream was theirs with all its hopes, expectations and anxieties, and the family firm was set fair for the future.

Just one year later the firm's turnover for the year 1904 topped the £7,000 mark. By the beginning of 1907 a further development was in the wind. Brewis & Co, a similar London firm of cutlers and silversmiths, had gone through various changes of ownership following the death of its founder William Brewis in 1891. When the opportunity presented itself Charles Fletcher started negotiations and early in 1907 he took over Brewis & Co. The following year he took the decision to form a limited company, and on 11th May 1908 he assigned his private business to C W Fletcher & Sons Ltd. At the end of World War One the company acquired larger premises at 76 Arundel Street, where they remain today.

With their expansion, Fletchers began for the first time to develop from supplying blanks to the trade to include the manufacture of the finished article: silver tea services, dishes, trays, coffee sets and many other items as well as complete canteens of cutlery.

In 1891 the enterprising young man set up in business, forging blanks for the cutlery trade. The rough blanks, made from solid silver and surprisingly heavy, were supplied by Fletchers to all the silversmiths in Sheffield for finishing.

The blanks were recognisable, certainly, as knives, forks and spoons - and though still very much in the rough at the same time possessed a solid and durable charm of their own. The blanks were forged with tangs in one solid piece, ready for mounting, so no extra soldering of handles was necessary at a later stage in the production process.

In 1899 Fletchers moved from their original premises, renting a factory in Bramall Lane which they named Sterling Works.

*Above: Indenture for C.W Fletcher to C.W Fletcher & Sons Ltd.*
*Right: C.W Fletcher & Sons Ltd Bramall Lane; workforce 1914.*

From ingot to finished hand-forged article took each piece through a number of processes before it reached completion: each piece of cutlery was forged, stamped, hand filed, buffed and finished by the company's team of skilled silversmiths. Some of the designs produced in the factory went back as far as the 18th century. The Rib Rattail, for example, with its clean, simple lines, was first made in the early 1700s and is still popular today. The Paul de Lamerie was a beautiful recreation of a design from 1746; De Lamerie was one of the world's great masters of craftsmanship and design. Onslow was a pattern produced around 1750 especially for Sir Arthur Onslow, who was speaker of the House of Commons between 1728 and 1761. Most of these early timeless designs are even now very much in fashion and are still being created today by C W Fletcher.

The process of creating an item of cutlery such as a spoon begins with a narrow bar of silver known as a slit. Shaped with the hammer alone, the blanks are produced by the forger with great skill. Each one is measured against a template as every individual spoon must be exactly the same size and thickness. Such is the skill of the Fletcher craftsman, the blank and the template match each other exactly.

By 1925 the company were manufacturing a much wider range of silverware: in addition to cutlery they made trophies, cups, flower stands, salad bowls, fruit

stands, cake baskets, shields, tea and coffee sets and much more. One of the original catalogues still survives, giving the price per set of 12 pairs of dessert knives and forks of around 14 ounces each as 2/9d per ounce. Among the many elegant designs illustrated are several ingenious folding pocket fruit knives with detachable knives and forks.

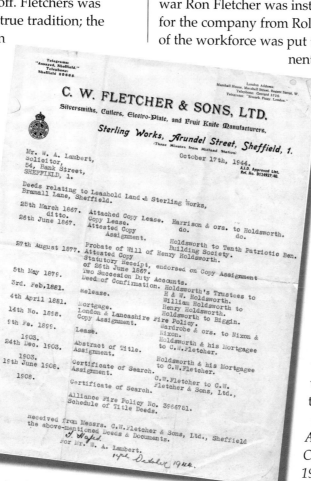

Charles Fletcher saw the company he had founded as a young man mature and flourish before he died in 1932 at the comparatively young age of 66. His three sons, Charles, Harold and William had followed him into the business, however, and were there to carry on where their father had left off. Fletchers was becoming a family firm in the true tradition; the young men each had their own expertise in the different aspects of the business. Harold, for example, was the company's representative. He would travel from town to town by railway, taking with him ten or so large packing cases full of samples of silver hollow ware and cutlery. With real entrepreneurial spirit he would rent a hotel room, hire a horse and cart to transport the cases of silverware from the station, and set up an attractive display in his room. Then he would visit prospective clients in the area and invite them to view the goods he had for sale. During the 1930s a further generation of the Fletcher family became involved in the company. Harold's son Ron had never visualised doing any other job and joined Fletchers as soon as he left school at the age of 14, to work with the flatware.

William Fletcher's son Eric took a position there in 1935 where he learned to produce hollow ware for the Company.

During the late 1930s, there were unsettling undercurrents at work, and the war that had been loomimg on the horizon for some time was looking inevitable as the decade wore towards its close. When war was finally declared in 1939, the production of silverware wound down as Fletchers' skilled workers were called on for the war effort.

The company changed direction, and from that time their main emphasis was on the engineering side of the business rather than the silverware. During the war Ron Fletcher was instrumental in winning orders for the company from Rolls Royce, and the expertise of the workforce was put to manufacturing components for the Merlin engine which was developed for the Spitfire and used on Lancaster bombers. Fletchers' small factory in London suffered in the blitz, and the only part of the building left undamaged was the office; work that was usually produced in London was transferred to Sheffield.

When it was clear that the war was almost over Fletchers once again set up their tooling and press work ready to go back to the manufacture of

*Above: Purchase receipt for C.W Fletcher from 6th august 1920. Left: Deeds relating to land and sterling works Bramwell Lane 8th Feb 1899. Facing page: Charlie Allcard, silver forger age 78.*

silverware. Fate dictated otherwise, however. Ron Fletcher had built up a close connection with Rolls Royce during the war and they invited Fletchers to carry on supplying their need for high precision fabricated components for their aircraft engines.

C W Fletcher's decision to go along this road was based on economics; the engineering was highly successful commercially, and silver was not so much so. From that time silverware took a much smaller part in the company's output, and eventually a separate company, C W Fletcher (Silversmiths) Ltd, was formed. They are one of the few surviving manufacturers of hand forged sterling silver flatware in Britain. Fletchers take pride in the fact that machinery is never used to roll and cut out their silver blanks. A machine could never achieve the subtle variation in thickness that each piece needs, and every item without exception is forged entirely by hand from the raw silver ingot.

Today, silver has been badly affected by imports from abroad, and Fletchers' largest orders for silverware come from the USA. They number among their customers some prestigious names such as Rockefeller and the Chase Manhattan Bank in New York.

The company is still trading today under Director Michael Rosewarne, who joined the firm in February 1957 as an apprentice silver forger. After having

progressed through the company, he was appointed as Manager in 1962.

During the post war years the engineering side of the business expanded with the boom in the aircraft industry, and Rolls Royce remained their prime clients. Rolls Royce gave them orders for Dart air intakes, which further strengthened C W Fletchers' expertise in fabricating aircraft components. Important links were forged with other leading manufacturers including The British Aircraft Corporation and MTU in Germany. In the 1950s the company expanded, and other buildings were constructed alongside the original premises to cope with the added demand for components. They invested in a further factory in Leadmill Street in 1957, which they developed into a large machine shop.

The company's high reputation for precision work resulted in their manufacture of a wide range of products including components for industrial gas turbines. Rolls Royce, in addition to their work in the aerospace industry, also had a nuclear division in Derby. Ron Fletcher was approached by them and asked to manufacture what they described as 'a special box'. The box they needed turned out to be a four foot long square tube designed to support nuclear fuel element rods. The job was a trial to assess the financial viability of the project and was destined for Harwell, the first reactor that was ever built in Britain. Ron took on the job. It was a turning point in the firm's history, and from then onwards C W Fletcher became involved with the atomic energy industry. They went on to win orders from British Nuclear Fuels for fuel sections for nuclear reactors in their power. The atomic energy industry is, of course, even more tightly controlled than the aircraft industry, and Fletchers' commitment to the highest levels of quality and craftsmanship has won them respect from every company with whom they have become involved.

It has not all been plain sailing for C W Fletcher & Sons, however. The company was still very much involved in the manufacture of aircraft components, and when Rolls Royce went down in 1971 the company suffered badly. Rolls Royce orders ceased and so did orders from other companies who were themselves dependent on Rolls Royce. At the time they had been taking on apprentices but as a result of Rolls Royces business disappearing, inside twelve months the number of apprentices had been reduced by half. In addition to that a number of Fletcher employees had to be made redundant, others left of their own accord. The company had a very tough

time during the years 1973-74. Eric and Ron Fletcher, as joint Managing Directors, made many personal sacrifices in order to keep the company viable, and the tremor was felt for a long time, even after Rolls Royce were helped out by the government. They were just beginning to make a slight recovery when world recession began to bite. Once more, redundancies had to be made. The company's workforce was severely depleted and did not fully recover until the late 1980's. Fletchers eventually went on to recover their losses, though only on paper, in real terms this was far from the case.

In 1986 the company was the first manufacturer of aircraft components to be awarded BS5750, which opened yet more doors, and they entered yet another new field when Lucas gave them orders for electrical containment equipment. At the same time their connection with Rolls Royce plc continued, and in 1986 Fletchers delivered the first components for Rolls Royce Tay and IAE V2500 engines. Further openings are being presented to the company, and in recent years a link with BMW Rolls Royce Gmb H has been established. Negotiating the contracts initially presented the executive staff at Fletchers with a lot of hard work and much travelling to and from Germany.

C W Fletcher & Sons' dedication to innovation and development led to a large investment in 1990 in computer aided design and computer aided manufac-turing (CAD/CAM), and in the direct numerical control of machine tools (DNC).

Ron Fletcher and Eric Fletcher retired in 1989 but stayed on the board, leaving joint Managing Directors Ray Louth and Brian Jenkinson to run the company, which today employs 144 workers and has a turnover of eight and a quarter million pounds.

And what of the future? Plans for further development are even now being implemented, and a site for a new one-storey factory and office development has been purchased in Waleswood, on the outskirts of Sheffield. The present factory in Arundel Street is to be sold and developed as part of Sheffield's Science and Cultural Industries quarter. The silverware business, however, as one of the city's traditional crafts, will probably remain in Arundel Street to form part of the Cultural Industries project.

Be that as it may, it is certain that the family firm who built their reputation on the impressive skills of their staff, the very best workmanship and painstaking attention to detail will continue to deliver more of the same to all their many and varied clients in the next Millennium.

*Above: Part of machine shop 1972.*
*Left: Fletcher's today, Sterling works, Arundel Street, Sheffield.*
*Facing page: Charlie Smart: Stamper, "Bowling Spoons" 1953.*

# Chocolate heaven since 1911

When commercial traveller Joseph William Thornton decided to quit the road and open a sweet shop, he was determined that his "Chocolate Kabin", should be the very best sweet shop in town. He opened his first shop in Norfolk Street Sheffield in 1911, and in those early days the family lived above the premises. Joseph's maxim was "Quality with high purity". Nearly 90 years on that is still the company's aim.

Unfortunately, when Joseph Thornton died in 1918 he was still relatively young. His two sons, Stanley and Norman, carried on the business. In 1920 they opened a shop in Rotherham - the first shop to be opened outside Sheffield, and four years later the Thorntons had a total of four shops.

Personalised confectionery is high on Thorntons list today, a trend which began many years ago when Stanley and Norman were making their very first Easter Eggs. The two young men came up with the idea of personalising the eggs, and began to ice the customers name on the egg while they waited. The idea was a great success, and the eggs were sold in "neat white boxes" for what was, even then, the reasonable sum of 4d each. Today, Thorntons shops ice more than two million names and other personal messages on Easter Eggs and chocolate products each year free of charge.

W.N.Thornton

Whilst Norman Thornton had a bent for marketing and retail, it was his younger brother Stanley who enjoyed experimenting with recipes. Thus the company began to manufacture and retail its own products from its early beginnings. The real breakthrough came when Stanley Thornton, in 1925, came up with a new and delicious recipe - "made with the best of everything" - what he called simply "Special Toffee". Before very long, Special Toffee was accounting for half the firm's sales. Then and now it is the company's policy to use only the finest ingredients, including sugar, milk, cream and dairy butter. An original fudge recipe still exists, and only granulated sugar, evaporated milk, butter and vanilla were used.

*Above:* W.Norman Thornton.
*Below:* All Saints Square, Rotherham.

ALL SAINTS SQUARE, ROTHERHAM.

Advertising from the time reveals that in those days you could buy milk assorted chocolates and chocolate nougats for 6d a quarter, while rum & butter toffees, butterscotch drops and assorted toffee cost 4d.

The company survived the 1920's recession with difficulty. Eight shops were opened by 1927 but these took only as much money as four had taken only a few years earlier. Norman and Stanley used to visit each shop late in the evening to collect the days takings in order to get these into the bank first thing the following morning, and they often used to remind the younger generation of those difficult days. From the early 1930's the company flourished and continued to expand, and more shops, mainly in Yorkshire and Lancashire,were opened. By the

mid 1930's a purpose built factory was required and the ultra modern Archer Road factory was opened in 1937. As well as up to date production facilities this included offices, stock holding facilities and a distribution centre. Thorntons' aim was to provide employee care and the factory was well ventilated and was lighted and heated by electricity - quite an innovation at the time. Employees had their own modem kitchen and dining room.

The Sheffield factory produced an amazing variety of sweets; a firm favourite with children was the range of chocolate animals. Another more unusual Thorntons' product was sugar coated halibut liver oil tablets which they developed especially for children, for "warding off ills and promoting health". The vitamin A and D content of the tablets reflected the general growing concern for children's health. Children's novelties still form part of the Thorntons range, with the cool characters Dottie Duck, Harvey Hog and Jake the Drake coming high on the list, together with Christmas Santas and Easter rabbits.

*Above: Charge Alley just before demolition.*
*Left: Thorntons first chocolate Kabin 1911, 159 Norfolk Street.*
*Right: Thorntons bill from 39,Churchton Street, 17.3.1955*

"Goodness!"

"It's Thorntons!"

Hand made chocolates and toffee delivered fresh every week

sophisticated of its kind in Europe, and its design has received awards for excellence.

The methods might have changed - but the old traditions still remain. Technology is complemented by traditional handcrafting. Thorntons Premier Collection, an exquisite luxury selection introduced to the range in 1995, includes many handcrafted chocolates; 18 carat gold leaf is applied by hand to each individual Champagne Créme chocolate.

Thorntons Special Toffee is still made in copper pans from Stanley's original recipe and poured by hand into special trays. Toffee is now automatically broken in the factory into bite sized pieces before being delivered on a weekly basis to each of the company's retail shops.

Today's distinctive "Taste of Thorntons" still reflects the policy of using only the best ingredients - a policy that has never changed. Thorntons chocolate contains high percentages of cocoa solids: the dark chocolate 60% and the milk chocolate 30%. Their careful attention to the quality of cocoa beans and other ingredients, and meticulous processing, ensures the chocolate's smooth texture and the flavour of the end product - a delight to chocoholics everywhere!

In 1954 Walter Willen, a young Swiss Confisseur, joined Thorntons, adapting authentic Swiss recipes to produce a delicious new range of distinctive chocolates. Thorntons Continental range has become the UK's top chocolate assortment. Now retired, Walter is still a consultant to the company. By the 1970's Thorntons had developed into Britain's leading specialist confectioners. Thorntons Continental range today includes Austrian, Swiss, Belgian and French inspired recipes, whilst the Italian selection recreates the flavours of the Mediterranean.

Whilst modern technology has been introduced many products are still hand finished. Today the company's chocolate manufacturing and distribution is handled from Thornton Park in Derbyshire, opened by Her Majesty the Queen in 1985. The production facility is one of the most

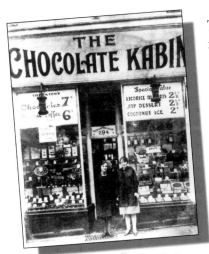

Today's global market place has added many new ingredients, textures and flavour combinations, and the distinctive Thornton recipes are created using the best fruits and marzipans, wines and liqueurs from around the world. Barry Colenso, former head patissier at the Savoy Hotel in London, now creates new Thorntons products and devises a variety of singular taste sensations to delight the customers.

Determined to provide as wide a range of products as possible, Thorntons produce a comprehensive range of chocolates, sweets and toffee developed especially for diabetics. A recent addition has been Thorntons Cooking Chocolate, made with 70% cocoa solids, and the pack includes two of Barry Colenso's recipes, for Petits Pots au Chocolat and a special Chocolate Sauce.

Something rather special was added to the Thorntons range in 1997 in the form of a new selection of larger than life American chocolates. Made to authentic American recipes and with typical transatlantic names such Awesome Chocolates, Florida Keys Pie, Golden Gate Slice, Big Apple, and even Cheerleader Bar, the new "candy" and chocolates which are "truly awesome"!.

Presentation is a big part of Thorntons commitment to excellence, shown by their stylish boxes and elegant packaging.

Christmas emphasises the "specialness" of Thorntons gifts: Dark Chocolate Gingers are presented in a special ceramic gift jar or in an elegant black and gold box, tiny snowmen and Santas have red ribbon hangers for hanging on the Christmas tree, and Special Toffee has its own ceramic pot.

The third generation of the Thornton family joined the company during the 1950's and 60's and in 1988 J W Thornton Ltd became Thorntons PLC when the company was floated on the London Stock Exchange. The 1990's saw Thorntons sales top £100 million, with over 500 UK shops planned for the new Millennium, together with up to 200 franchise outlets for the smaller towns and city suburbs.

Joseph Williain's grandsons John and Michael Thornton are now the firm's Chairman and Deputy Chairman and their ambition, like that of their grandfather Joseph William, is to have "the nicest sweet shop in town".

*Facing Page top: Thornton's first advert from the late 1920's. Facing Page bottom: The lorry at the Belper factory in the 1970's with its old logostyle and Three Chefs motif. Above: Prewar, 1 London Road, Sheffield, a temporary shop during the World War 11 through the Blitz. Below: One of Thorntons two shops at Meadowhall, Sheffield. This is Thorntons most successful shopping centre where the company has shops on both the ground floor and upper levels.*

# *Marsdens - Food for thought*

Just over three quarters of a century ago, Mr A T Marsden, a young man of 22 was working as a farm boy for forty shillings a week. He was born in the Hope Valley, Derbyshire, he came from a farming family and expected, when he left school, to find work on the family farm.

When the time came, however, he found that because farming was at a very low ebb, this meant hard work and little reward. Nor did he think matters would improve a great deal in the foreseeable future. He was a prudent young man who had saved 15s a week out of his 40s pay as well as handing over the money for his board and lodging.

Now he had £100 saved, which in the twenties was enough to make a fresh start. It seemed to him that the dairy industry had better prospects and so he bought a retail dairy business operating from

the Hope Valley. He sold his milk in Sheffield, just 14 miles away whilst at the same time developing the wholesale side of the business. He found the dairy industry in 'an extremely chaotic state'. Later, the Milk Marketing Board would sort it out.

The ice-cream department of Mr Marsden's business came to be because he was ending each day's retail selling with a surplus of milk. To begin with, he sold it to other ice-cream manufacturers but soon decided that it would be more profitable to make his own.

By now he was selling his milk from his dairy at Sandygate in Sheffield. He put in a small vertical brine freezer there, and to begin with he produced between twenty and thirty gallons a week. From 1933 and 1935, Mr Marsden sold milk in the mornings and ice-cream in the afternoons. Then he heard that a milk bar had been opened in Fleet Street, London and liked the idea. Encouraged by the Milk

Marketing Board which was keen on any scheme that would further the sale of milk, he opened his own milk bar in Pinstone Street in Sheffield.

By the mid fifties he had opened five of them in Sheffield, Bawtry and Rotherham.

During the war, he had to close down his ice-cream making department and turn his hand to farming again. He had 600 acres of his own and helped his brother to run another 1,000 acres.

*Facing page:* Reprint from the February, 1954 issue of *"The Ice Cream Industry"*.
*Facing page bottom:* First delivery vehicle.
*This page:* Confectionary, the poster on the door dates 2nd April 1962.
*Below:* Jimmy James at the Empire opening occasion of the first milk bar.

After the war he continued his farming interests but returned to his milk-related business. In 1946, the firm opened the Carlton Restaurant in Sheffield and the Carlton Hotel and Restaurant in Cleethorpes. When the ban on the sale of ice-cream was lifted, Mr Marsden set about modernising his factory. Together with some colleagues he attended an ice-cream convention in America and inspected a number of factories. He came back with many new ideas to incorporate into his own, and by the mid fifties his production capabilities rose to 250,000 gallons a year.

His factory was a model for all to see, with its three cold rooms, two 120-gallon continuous freezers. two pasteurisers. cooler, four ageing vats and various compressors.

At this point, Mr Marsden decided to give up the retail side of the dairy business and give more time to his restaurants, farms, milk and snack bars and the ice-cream trade. Staff at the factory and his other establishments numbered 200. For ice-cream distribution to outlets as far afield as the east coast he used a fleet of delivery vans ranging from 10cwts to three tonners. He also operated a number of permanent and mobile kiosk points in sheffield and its environs, and managed a cafeteria and ice-cream kiosks in popular Clumber Park. Ice-cream products included gateaux, ice-cream cakes and lollies. the favourite flavours were vanilla, strawberry and chocolate.

The sixties brought further diversification as the company began to operate fast food units, hotels, pubs and more restaurants. This side of the business developed quickly and over the next couple of decades most of the company's previous concerns were phased out. Units within the Marsden Group by 1980 comprised the Four Restaurants, Arundel Gate, the Dore Grill, the Maynard Arms Hotel at Grindleford, the Fox Hotel, Brotherton, three more hotels at Matlock, the Snake Pass and Highfields, together with the Wimpy Bar in Pinstone Street and the Pop-In in the High Street in Rotherham. In this year, the Marsden Group's in-house magazine, 'Food for Thought' was launched.

The Flagship for 1970 was an 80 bedroomed hotel, "The Wetherby Turnpike" it flourished for 10 years before Marsdens sold it in 1980. In 1981 Stephanie Connelly (Catering) Ltd was acquired to operate future fast food development and two Kentucky Fried Chicken stores were taken over by the company. This is a franchise operation originally begun in the USA by a Colonel Sanders. In 1981 a single piece of chicken cost 45p whilst £1 58p bought three pieces of chicken with chips.

Currently the company has nine Kentucky Fried Chicken Units and one restaurant in Arundel Gate in Sheffield. All are successfully administered from the headquarters which are to be found still at the company's original premises at Sandygate which had been the Marsden family home until 1944.

*Above: Staff in the first milk bar.*
***Facing page bottom:*** *Shop window of Marsdens caterers.**Facing page top:** Marsdens Sandygate shop and delivery van.*

# Brownill Vickers - specialists in the valuation and sale of licensed property

Walking along Queen Street today and pausing to look at the properties advertised in the window of number 82 only those 'in the know' would appreciate the amount of history connected with Surveyors, Valuers and Estate Agents Brownill Vickers. There are few such firms in the city who can trace their heritage back to 1884 and fewer still who can boast that their offices occupy the very site their founder utilised when setting up business at that time. The fact that, although now representing a general practice firm of valuers, auctioneers, surveyors and estate agents dealing with all classes of property, their historical specialisation in a niche market has led to Brownill Vickers becoming one of the largest firms of Licensed Property specialists in the country makes the company's history all the more interesting.

which had specialised in all aspects of licensed property valuation for over a century, Brownills and Hartle Sons & Vickers.

The roots of these two firms go back to the 1870's when a certain Charles Day made a name for himself as the foremost licensed property valuer in the area. His work would have included finding tenants for around twenty breweries in the region and valuing pub fixtures, fittings and stocks when one publican left and another took over.

He was regarded as being something of a celebrity and it would not be uncommon for him to be rewarded not only with his fee but with the traditional dinner of his choice served to him by the outgoing publican on the day of the 'changeover'.

Brownill Vickers was formed in 1989 as the result of a merger between two firms

Over the years, Charles Day, gave guidance to a number of young men in the profession of hotel valuing and no less than five of these ultimately set up their own business in competition (William Brownill, Joseph Henry Hartle, Arthur Smith, John Greenwood and Turner Wilson). Each went on to conduct their own businesses for many years but it is Brownill

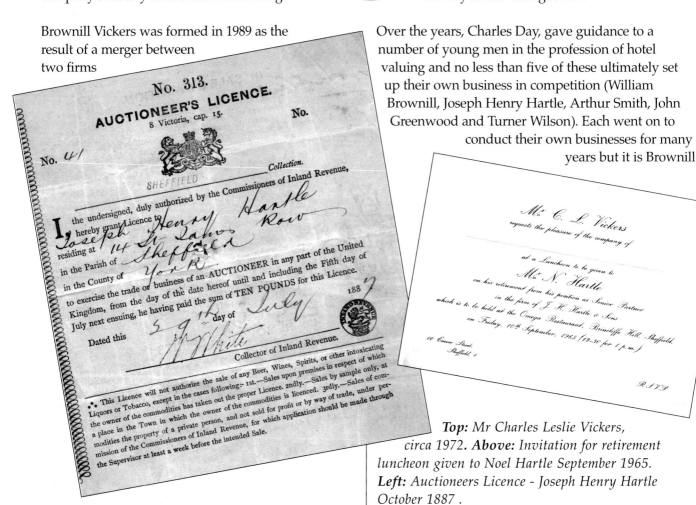

**Top:** *Mr Charles Leslie Vickers, circa 1972.* **Above:** *Invitation for retirement luncheon given to Noel Hartle September 1965.* **Left:** *Auctioneers Licence - Joseph Henry Hartle October 1887 .*

(establishing his company in 1884) and Hartle (1887) we are interested in for the purpose of this article.

There became a surfeit of licensed property valuers in the area in the late 19th century leading to each of them finding it to be increasingly difficult to earn a living. Subsequent directory entries list Charles Day as being a pig dealer and this would suggest that in countering such competition 'the mentor' changed his line of work.

Joseph Henry Hartle was killed during the First World War. His widow Alice was not trained to continue the business and had to care for her two young sons, Noel and Joseph (Jnr). She therefore sold the records and files of her late husband's firm to William Brownill. Alice Hartle continued to collect rents for a limited income and waited for her sons to mature. When, Noel Hartle, by now in his early twenties, recommended pub valuations with his brother Joe as a sleeping partner under the title of J.H. Hartle & Sons, William Brownill protested on the grounds that having purchased the records and files of his main competitors he had effectively bought his rival's company. His claim was not upheld.

In 1924, Noel Hartle took on Leslie Vickers, a boy of fourteen, to help his mother Alice look after the office.

This consisted of an attic in Bank Street over the well known newsagents and stationers H. Turner & Son. Cramped (and in the summer very hot) accommodation and, following demolition of the original buildings, now part of "the Corporation" and "the Other Side" night club venues.

William Brownill died leaving the business in the hands of his partner, Charles Webster and his son John (known as Johnty). Problems arose in 1942 when Webster died whilst John Brownill was still serving the RAF in North Africa. A. E. Wilbey & Son of Barnsley took over Brownill and Webster and in fact were current longest serving Partner's David Fleetwood's first employers in 1950.

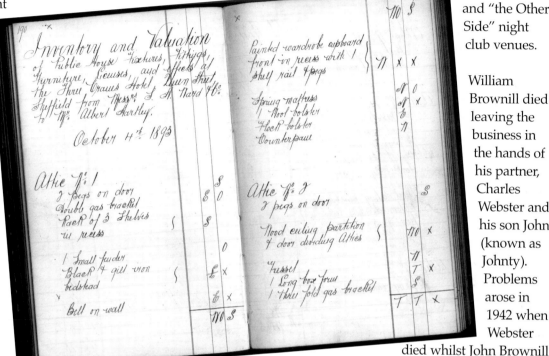

*Above: Valuation book relating to calculations concerning several valuations carried out by William Brownill in 1893. Below: A staff photograph from the 1987 centenary celebrations of Hartle Sons & Vickers.*

It took John Brownill, on returning to England after the war, some time to re-establish himself but he eventually re-purchased the family business recommencing trading with David Fleetwood as Brownill and Webster in 1956. Alistair Firth, son of the firms then Bank Manager, joined the business as an articled clerk in 1969.

Now aged 86 Leslie Vickers remembers that the 15 shillings a week he was paid at Hartle and Sons in 1924 represented a welcome improvement on the 10 shillings he was receiving from his previous employers the Albion Motor Company. However, he objected to having to call Noel Hartle 'Sir' and to being on call seven days a week without any overtime pay. Unfit for military service he was required during the Second World War to become involved in specialist accountancy for the licensed trade and to do monthly audits at the Gaumont British Bars. Later, the Board of Trade insisted that 'Hartles' should settle a good number of war damage claims, including the Marples Hotel, Fitzalan Square. These became a profitable source of income.

The scramble for jobs just after the war led to an influx of a number of 'undesirables' into the business. Local breweries reacted by virtually compelling 'approved' establishments to form an organisation which became known as the Society of Sheffield and District Licensed Property Valuers. This was established in 1944 with Leslie Vickers as its Secretary.

In 1947 J.H Hartle and Sons moved to Tontine Chambers on the corner of Dixon Lane and Haymarket over Montague Burtons shop. Leslie's son Rodger joined the company in 1964 and remembers trying to concentrate on his work whilst 'big Ada', the flower vendor on Dixon Lane, yelled 'flowers bob a bunch'. His starting wage was £4.00 out of which he had to pay 6 shillings tax.

By this time Leslie Vickers had become rather than had been made a partner in J.H. Hartle and Sons. Noel Hartle retired in 1965 and the firm became Hartle Sons and Vickers with Leslie Vickers as principal. The development of Peter Stringfellow's Nightclub (the Penthouse) on Dixon Lane meant the firm had to relocate its offices to Alpha House, Carver Street. (Originally a cutlery factory).The business was fast expanding into general, commercial and residential property and needed a ground floor position. Hartle Sons and Vickers moved to shop premises at 175 West Street in 1980.

In the meantime Brownill and Webster had taken over another old established firm of valuers in the city - Cooper Sons and Spencer with a view to relocating in Spencer's offices on the opposite side of the road for a short time whilst 82 Queen Street was completely re-built to the form as it stands today. The company was retitled Brownill Spencer and Fleetwood and were by now, along with Hartle Sons and Vickers be the only specialised licensed property valuers within the city - competition between them was extremely intense. In 1989 a major decision was made - it was thought that the energy expended in each of the firms outwitting one another would be better spent in pooling their

*Above left:* A busy day on the Haymarket in the Sheffield city centre. The Dixon Lane offices of Hartle & Sons can be seen on the second floor at the top left of the picture.
*Right:* Brownill's advertisement in the Worksop and Retford Brewery Almanac of 1896.

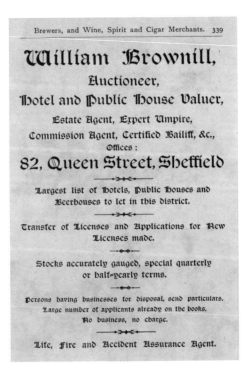

Brewers, and Wine, Spirit and Cigar Merchants. 339

**William Brownill,**
Auctioneer,
Hotel and Public House Valuer,
Estate Agent, Expert Umpire,
Commission Agent, Certified Bailiff, &c.,
Offices :
**82, Queen Street, Sheffield**

Largest list of Hotels, Public Houses and Beerhouses to let in this district.

Transfer of Licenses and Applications for New Licenses made.

Stocks accurately gauged, special quarterly or half-yearly terms.

Persons having businesses for disposal, send particulars. Large number of applicants already on the books. No business, no charge.

Life, Fire and Accident Assurance Agent.

resources, intellectual and practical, and the firms merged in 1989 to become Brownill Vickers. The current partners, David Fleetwood, Rodger Vickers, Alistair Firth, John Jenkinson and Miles Pierce and Miles Pierce (all partners in the merged firm in 1989) are now supplemented by three associates, two consultants and twenty four various members of staff providing a comprehensive service to all connected with the property profession.Whilst the licensed trade aspect of the business continues to be important the modern Brownill Vickers can best be described as a general practice firm of valuers, surveyors and agents dealing with all classes of residential and commercial property.

Brownill Vickers are proud of the service they have been able to afford to the people of Sheffield and its companies over the past one hundred and fourteen years and approach the millennium with confidence.

*Above: Current offices of Brownill Vickers. **Top Left:** Noel and Norah Hartle at the time of their wedding in the 1950's. **Top right:** Brownill's centenary in 1984 - David Fleetwood (on the left), John "Johnty" Brownill in the centre and Alistair Firth on the right. **Left:** Four of the current partners of Brownill Vickers at their 1998 annual luncheon - from the left Rodger Vickers, David Fleetwood, Miles Pierce, Alistair Firth, Edwina Curry (guest speaker) and John Palmer (consultant, Chester Office).*

# History in the baking

George Henry Fletcher was not a Sheffield man, being born in 1878 in Horncastle. He began his working life as a farm labourer, later coming as a baker to Ostler's Mill which ground its own corn, then used its own flour in its bakery. Since the flour came in 15-stone sacks, bakers needed good muscles.

He and his wife Kate suffered many misfortunes as they tried to raise a family. Their dire poverty drove Mr Fletcher to become an active member of the Bakers' Union and join enthusiastically in their fight for a 60-hour week. Because of his union activities, he was blacklisted by employers and had no choice but to set up in business on his own. Having no capital, he began by baking for individual households locally.

A shortage of imported flour during the First world War meant queues outside the Attercliffe bakeries. Fletchers had their first mechanical aid, an Artofex dough mixer, installed in 1915 and soon afterwards acquired a Model T Ford for deliveries.

Meanwhile he was becoming something of a local hero from his championship of workers' rights and his business efforts were supported. So much so that, by 1923, he was able to open a new bakery in the reasonably prosperous area of Middlewood Road, Hillsborough. He was determined to run his business on egalitarian principles and to improve the conditions within the bakery industry as a whole.

His son, George junior, who had little luck in his career as a mechanic, joined him and the two men took the bread they had baked on a barrow to sell in the street. As George senior had become a local hero as a political champion of the poor they flocked to buy from him and business flourished.

By 1926 Fletchers' 6th bakery opened in Peniston Road. It was equipped with a 2-deck Baker Perkins oven, revolutionary progress for those times. By 1936 there were 11 large red vans. Every machine in every bakery was George junior's concern.

engineer at a time when technology was the key to advance. Paul's talents were organisational. He took a an overall look at the bakery and kept an eye on all that was happening in the baking world outside, picking up the best ideas and innovations. Fletchers were therefore the first bakers in Europe to introduce a Lanham plant. It cost £500,000 and produced 14,000 burger buns an hour. automation gradually took over most processes.

By 1991 Fletchers was offering an extensive range of frozen foods whilst the Claywheels Lane Bakery produced six million doughnuts, scones and burger buns a week. However, the nineties brought the decision to close all Fletchers' high street shops including the flagship outlet in Exchange Street. Freezer plants had been introduced in 1983 making it possible for the company to sell nationwide.

The staff are as well treated as they were by the original George, being amongst the best-paid in the industry. A reluctant decision to close the wholesale Department was made in 1998 which was then only 5% of the turnover but the management was delighted that it was achieved without any enforced redundancies.

After the second Sheffield Blitz there was a bakery fire, due to an employee's error rather than Hitler. George was undismayed, commenting, "It was about time we had a clear-out." It was the spirit in which he regarded the business until his death in 1858 at the age of 79.

The 7th bakery was in Claywheels Lane. George junior noticed the ideal site when he took his son Paul sledging at Wadsley Bridge. He bought it in 1947.

In the 70s bread demand dropped. The discount war began, but the company resisted takeover bids from bigger bakeries. Sliced bread was in demand and bagging machines for it caused Fletchers more problems than any other piece of machinery. Entry into the Common Market increased the price of flour because of punitive levies on North American wheat. Fletchers retained 50% of Canadian wheat in their flour and continued making 'open confectionery' when other firms resorted to prepacked.

On George Fletcher's death in 1973 the business came to his son Paul. George had been an inspired

Paul Fletcher has announced his intention to retire in the year 2,000. The firm is likely to be taken over by Northern Foods.

**Top:** *The Middlewood Road shop which fronted onto the thoroughfare and a bakehouse.*
**Bottom:** *Claywheels Lane works, the seventh bakery.*
**Facing page top:** *Left to right: George, George Henry, Paul. Three generations taken in the early 1950's.*
**Facing page bottom:** *Fletchers, large red vans from 1936.*

# Serving the country through the war

The company, Atkinson Walker (Saws) Ltd has its roots in the former firm of Colver Brothers Ltd of the Pilot Works. In 1920, this firm was incorporated with the Neepsend Steel & Tool Corporation, and its saw department was moved in with Slack Sellers & Company Ltd. Unhappy with this situation, Messrs R H and J Walker and Mr H Tingle left the old company and set up as saw manufacturers as Walker, Son & Tingle.

When John Walker served in the forces during the First World War, he spent his time maintaining the saws and equipment of the Royal Engineers' Saw Mills in France. With this experience, in limited accommodation in Wellmeadow Street, he did much of the work when the new company was formed in November 1923.

Until the general slump in 1926, the business grew steadily, outgrowing its premises in 1924 when a

move was made to Charlotte Lane. The previous leaseholders, also saw manufacturers, now bankrupt, had left behind a well lit smithing shop and a saw hardening furnace. During the period 1930-33 the annual turnovers were lower than in the first years of trading. Mr Tingle retired and was bought out of the business which became R H Walker & Son Limited. Having named their premises the Falcon Works, the Walkers registered the trade mark Falcon with the Sheffield Cutlers' Company which became an established name throughout the saw trade in England.

From the beginning, Edward Peace & Company had done Walkers' grinding. In 1932 this business came on

*Above:* Richard Henry Walker with Son & Grandsons shortly before his death in 1940. *Below:* Left to right H Tingle, J Walker, R.H Walker. 78 inch diameter saw probably destined for a sawmill in Africa.

the market. Walkers bought it and carried it on as a separate profit making company until 1940 when it was amalgamated with the parent firm. Now Walkers had their own grinding facilities whilst Peace's paid its own way, bringing a small indirect profit to the company.

The Union Grinding Wheel used by Edward Peace & Company was unfortunately situated at some distance from the Falcon Works and the saws had to be transported to and from it on a handcart However, the lease on the property was due to expire and an increase in business by 1937 made larger premises necessary.

A site was taken on Cotton Mill Row and plans were made for a new modern factory and offices. Using just half the land, Walkers put up a hardening shop, a machine shop, a smithing shop, a warehouse and two offices. The new compact factory, erected on the Alma Street end of the plot, was close at hand to the grinding wheel. The new building was given the name of the old one, the Falcon works.

*Above: Sandstone grinding.*
*Right: Circular saw toothing.*

At this auspicious time, John Walker junior joined the company.

The government re-armament programme at the end of the thirties brought an increase in trade. When war was declared in September 1939, John Walker's younger son Robert joined the firm. That year, a Churchill type of rotary magnetic chuck was bought for the new machine shop. It enabled saws to be evenly ground to a thousandth of an inch and left a

respectable-looking finish without any need for glazing. It also did hollowgrinding and bevelling of circular knives.

On the death of Mr R H Walker in 1940, his son became Chairman of the company and John junior became a director. As the demands of the war on the company increased, more new equipment was bought. Later in the war, John Walker bought the controlling interest in Messrs George Atkinson & Company, a Cardiff firm that made bandsaws. Walkers expanded the company with the aid of plentiful labour available in Wales so that it could also produce other types of saws, including handsaws.

In 1942 Robert Walker joined the Royal Navy, leaving Johns, father and son, to run the factory. They replanned the machine shop, motorising each machine separately. More improvements were necessary to keep pace with the flow of orders. The hardening shop was given a coal-fired tempering furnace with two 42" diameter dies. They made the saws much flatter for smithing and gave greater output because the temperature of the hardening furnace no longer had to be lowered for tempering.

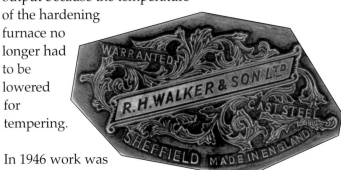

In 1946 work was begun on a new grinding wheel on the south side of the land and other work was done, necessary to the formation of a compact small saw grinding shop. It was expected that the number of orders would fall when the war ended and plans were made to increase the number of products the company sold abroad. Agents were appointed throughout the world, all of whom found plenty of demand for saws.

However, demand in the home market did not slacken and it was difficult to supply foreign markets. It was decided to deal mainly in Australia and New Zealand and a considerable business was built up with these two countries. New Zealand, in particular, wanted the smaller sizes of circular saws which could be almost mass-produced by the new machines with which John Walker had recently equipped his factory.

In 1947, Robert Walker returned from the war and was made a director. He took more responsibility in Sheffield, leaving his father free to give time to the rapidly growing associate company in Cardiff.

The new grinding wheel was completed. It was the last of the plans for improvement that had been made when the land in Cotton Mill Row had been first leased, but by 1948 it was apparent that even further extension was necessary. Demobilised men had been trained as smithers and the company's six anvils were now insufficient. New land was leased south of the grinding wheel and a new smithing shop was built on the foundations of a firewood factory that had stood on the new site. An existing garage was converted into a hardening shop for small circular saws.

When all the new building was completed, experiments were carried out to find a substitute for the whale oil used in quenching. A straight blend of

*Above: Acid etch mark for circular saws introduced in the 1930's.*
*Left: 1920's quenching a 48 inch saw blade from the hardening furnace.*

mineral oil was found to be suitable which could be bought from the Anglo American Oil Company at a quarter of the price of whale oil.

In 1950 steel became more plentiful so that it was possible to get up to date with orders. However, a new defence programme at the end of the year meant that soon production was again being held up for lack of steel.

By 1954 it was decided to close the Cardiff factory, consolidating the handsaw and bandsaw manufacturing with the circular saw production in Sheffield. To make room for it the existing Sheffield factory was once again enlarged and the Rifle Tavern on Bower Street was purchased and demolished. The old-fashioned grinding machines, fairly recently put in now became recognised as a health risk and in any case it was difficult to obtain the sandstones they required. In 1957 the old machines were replaced by a Lumsden vertical spindle segmental grinder with a 36″ diameter magnetic chuck. In future, since the demand for larger saws had reduced, it was decided to produce them only to a maximum diameter of 36″. This left room for precision grinders to be brought in which allowed the company to produce a better balanced and accurate saw blade.

John Walker's son in law, Bill Perry who had been a director of the Cardiff firm became director in charge of handsaw production until his retirement in 1981. Meanwhile, up until the mid seventies, modernisation of production methods continued. They included gas fired furnaces, an electrically heated tempering goff, automatic toothing machines and the commencement of injection moulding of handsaw handles with the handle being moulded directly on to the blade.

The installation of compressed air all round the factory had major effects, not least being the operation of clutches on presses with interlocks to conform to new regulations.

During 1981 the Company introduced the production of tungsten carbide tipped saw blades. These were so well received by customers that a major investment programme was required to cope with demand for the new products. Their reputation for these high quality precision saw blades has continued to spread to the extent Atkinson-Walker has become one of the leading UK manufacturers of such products and 75% of output is now accounted for by them.

As John and Robert Walker retired from the scene, control was taken on by Robert's three sons, Chris,

Fraser and Andrew. They have forged ahead with new products to ensure that the firm which has survived in the saw trade for nearly eighty years will continue to have a very viable future.

As the two companies of Atkinson and R H Walker merged, the names were contracted to the present title, Atkinson Walker (Saws) Limited.

The 1990s have seen rapid change in the markets supplied by Atkinson Walker (Saws) Limited. In contrast to the first 65 years, when the company's products were primarily supplied to the UK market and traditional Commonwealth countries, during the last decade there has been a rapid expansion in international demand for Atkinson-Walkers' circular saws and hand tools. This has resulted in exports to every continent and 50 countries around the world.

Modernisation in the production processes has been blended in with the traditional saw making skills. Incorporated into the on-going investment programme are further developments in automation and robotics for blade handling and loading and modern precision grinding equipment for even higher standards.

Due to a shortage of space for expansion, the freehold to Globe Steel Works and adjacent former cottages on Alma Street was acquired in 1991. Although in a poor state of repair, phase 1 of their renovation was completed in July 1998 with the reroofing of the main building and restoration of the Globe on the facia to its former glory as a prominent landmark to the Kelham Island area of Sheffield.

Whilst change is necessary and desirable for future excellence, many of the original objectives of the founder, Richard Henry Walker for quality, service and value are still valid after nearly 80 years and will be upheld by future generations of Walkers.

*Left*: *This page is taken from R.H Walker & Son Ltd leaflet in 1964.*
***Below:*** *Former and current directors of Atkinson - Walker (Saws) Ltd, on completion of renovation of Globe Steel Works - July 1998* ***Facing page:*** *Tempering Goff for circular saws up to 42" diameter.*

# A permanent fixture

After serving his apprenticeship with J & E Ison of Ashby-de-la-Zouch, George Williams moved to Sheffield in 1875, to take charge of Walker and Hall's showrooms. He was just 23 years old. As his father had been a skilled cordwainer, George's background had largely been in boot manufacturing, but in that same year the enterprising young man set up in business in Norfolk Street with his brother Edward as brass founders and general merchants. They dealt in steel files, spring bolts and nuts, nails, screws and aluminium, as well as being agents for firebricks and pot clays. The year before he established his business George had married Helen Hurst from Northwich, Cheshire. He was destined to become the father of quite a large family. The couple's first child, Rowland, was born in 1880, the oldest of six children.

In 1877 Williams Brothers moved to premises in Green Lane, Kelham Island, a site conveniently situated in the heart of Sheffield's industrial area, acquiring the stock, plant and debts of an already well established firm. The old building was believed to have once been a coaching inn - a belief which seems to be borne out by the atmospheric rooms and little winding stairways - and by the firm's resident ghost! For many years, even after the building became in turn part of the office complex, a mess room and a shower room for the men, members of staff would experience what they could only describe as the odour of a horse which had been ridden hard. Though none of them ever reported seeing anything out of the ordinary, it was their belief that this block had once been the inn's stables, and had been used as a changing post for fresh horses on a long journey.

A ghostly presence was also felt in a room at the top of the building. Tucked away under the roof, the room was especially eerie on dark winter days, and many of the staff were reluctant to go there.

A flight of stone steps lead from the yard to the cellar, where a network of underground tunnels once ran below the streets of the town. Rumour has it that the local villains used the tunnels to move contraband between the local inns.

The dubious history of the building had no detrimental effect on the company, however, and Williams brothers started to show a profit. Two years after moving to Green Lane they announced a profit of £800. 18s. 5d, and in 1890 they acquired No 38 Green Lane.

In those early years, when deliveries were made by horse and cart, local people were used to seeing Williams Brothers flat carts around the streets.

The horses were reputed to know the delivery run so well that if a driver fell asleep with the reins in his hands, the horse would get him back around the well-known streets, through the archway and into Williams Brothers cobbled yard. The advent of the motor lorry saw the end of the magnificent animals (not to mention seeing an end to the idea of nodding off in the driving seat!).

George Williams himself became a well-known figure in the area. At the time of his death at the early age of 52 he was a keen member of the Eccleshall Conservative Association and a member of the Broomgrove Bowling Club, being appointed president just a year before his death. He was also a regular church-goer, attending St Mark's Church on a regular basis, and only a short time before he died in 1905 he retired from the post of church-warden.

The company that George Williams established was a family firm in the true tradition - in fact Philip Williams, great-grandson of founder George Williams, is today the firm's Chairman.

Through the years, many of the firm's employees have also been whole families, with husbands and wives, fathers and mothers, brothers, sisters and cousins, working together. In those days few school leavers joined the ranks of the unemployed; qualifications were unnecessary - if they could write their name they simply joined their family at Williams Brothers, and the rest moved along to accommodate the newcomer.

In 1919 the firm took another step forward and became a limited company, Williams Brothers (Sheffield) Limited.

With the onset of hostilities in 1939 the engineering department began to flourish, and throughout World War II continued to aid the war effort. Their expansion continued after the war, and a new warehouse block was built between 1947-48, making good use of the Bridgehouses railway station as well as the traditional horse and cart.

The 1960's saw the final years of the brass foundry the opening of new offices, and the appointment as a main GKN distributor.

*This page: Foundry tools 1922. **Facing page top:** Account books from 1880 and 1904. **Facing page bottom:** William Brothers transportation in August 1922.*

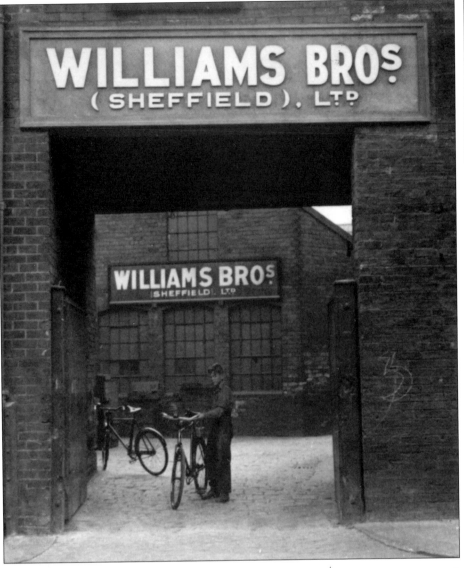

Down the years Williams Brothers has been ready to respond to the changing needs of the market place, establishing a track record for providing a first class service to their customers. The company put their phenomenal success down to a combination of their friendly and knowledgeable workforce, who are always ready to offer advice, the quality of their service, the ready availability of their stock, and their ability to tailor-make non-stock items to a client's order. Small quantities can be produced from a client's drawings or samples, and stock items can be modified to suit, with extra thread, shortening or drilling.

Williams Fasteners, as it is known today, pride themselves on servicing Blue Chip companies on a national basis in the steel, mining and utility industries. With a customer base of over 3000, ranging as far afield as Cornwall and Scotland in the UK, as well as worldwide in Canada and India.

All these elements have played their part in the development of Williams Fasteners.

In an ongoing drive for constant improvement in customer service, staff training is high on their agenda. Staff tend to stay with the company, and clients can still deal directly with employees who have been with Williams Fasteners for upwards of twenty years, with less than ten years service being considered a new boy.

From 1993 the company has undergone dramatic expansion, with a turnover that went from £3 million to around £8 million, capturing a number of large national contracts. The company celebrated the new year of 1997 with a major expansion, buying out Anfast, a fastenings distributor based in Norwich. This enabled them to focus on supplying the needs of customers within a forty mile radius of the premises, and gave them the opportunity to add further specialist products to their range and to tap into new markets.

The ever increasing number of customers in the East Yorkshire area led to the opening of a further branch in Hull, in 1997. Until that time the Sheffield premises had serviced the Humberside region, and the setting up of the new branch meant that operations could be run more efficiently. Ever to the forefront in new developments, the company installed a new £150,000 computer network that would enable them to increase their efficiency still further by co-ordinating the sales and stock-holding activities of other branches that were being opened.

In the same year Williams Fasteners transferred its head office and delivery depot from Green Lane to their present headquarters in Shepcote Lane, Tinsley. The new premises included a 30,000 sq ft warehouse and 6000 sq ft of offices that allowed the firm to keep over £1m of stock.

Today, they also have premises in the East Midlands and in Manchester, offering a range of more than 50,000 items - screws, nuts, bolts, washers and rivets of every kind, which can be ready for delivery the same day.

A recent development that complements their tele-sales service has been the setting up of the company's web site, which means that finding information about the firm's products and ordering stock can be done simply and conveniently. At the click of a mouse their extensive portfolio can be made available to potential clients. Internet orders are promptly dealt with by staff at the Tinsley headquarters.

Keeping abreast of new developments and markets has kept the Company in the forefront, and today they are finding that investment and expansion is paying off - which goes to show that the sense of challenge established by George Williams almost 130 years ago is still very much alive and well today.

It is with great sadness that Philip Williams passed away whilst this history was still in its proof stages, however there is no intention to give up 130 years of history that easily, and Williams Fasteners will continue under family control.

This article is written in memory and honour of Philip D. Williams.

*Above: Philip Williams (Chairman) in their 30,000 sq ft warehouse, with managing director George Earle.*
*Bottom: Early product supplies made by William Brothers.*
*Facing page above left: Williams Bros premises in the early part of the century.*
*Facing page above right: Williams Bros billboard stating that it was established in 1875. Facing page bottom: This Transport dates back to the early 1970's*

# Packing them in for more than a century

The long history of Greenups Packaging spans around 120 years. Around 1910 the firm moved to Wellington Street, Sheffield, where they operated as a general commercial printer. Among their clients in the summer of 1911 was Sheffield Corporation, who before the municipal printing works were established commissioned outside printers to do their work. Greenup and Thompson did most of the Corporation die-stamping at that time.

When Sheffield Corporation gave the firm an order for 50,000 copies of their Coronation Programme Booklet in 1911, it was a case of 'all hands on deck'. Working to a tight deadline the entire staff, including the office workers, put everything they had into the task, working long hours to get the Coronation Programmes ready on time. Needless to say, the hard work paid off and the job was completed on schedule, and the Managing Director, Mr J Williams, decided to say thank you to his staff

for all their hard work by treating the entire workforce to a day out in the country. The 'Old Time Coaches', hired from a well known Sheffield firm, drove them out to the Strines Inn, the young ladies and girls in their summery hats and best skirts and blouses, the men debonair in suits and straw boaters. The meal they had at the inn stayed in their memories for a long time; a former employee remembered that they were served with home fed ham and eggs, bread and butter and a sweet. In a day when workers were able to enjoy few pleasure trips, this unexpected outing was a red letter day. The meal cost the firm 1/6d per head - a fact that no doubt added to the employees' pleasure!

The two world wars were difficult for Greenups, as those years were for most companies. A number of the staff served in the military and some were lost in active duty. A framed memorial commemorates those lost in World War One. The premises suffered bomb damage in the second world war.

The company remained at Wellington Street until 1963, and by that time they were offering a range of services, including colour printing - in fact for many years they printed the programmes for both of Sheffield's football clubs. Labels, stationery and wrappers for the local razor blade industry were among their regular contracts. Carton making by this time figured largely among their services, and in the early 1970s they took the important decision to concentrate entirely on printed packaging.

In 1968 British Syphon Industries purchased the company, and in 1977 they moved to a purpose-built factory which gave them the opportunity to concentrate on carton printing.

In 1984 the company underwent a further change when the directors undertook a management buyout.

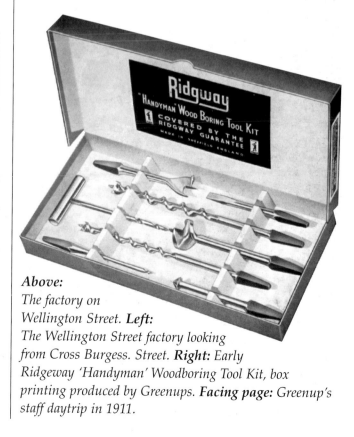

*Above:*
*The factory on*
*Wellington Street.* **Left:**
*The Wellington Street factory looking*
*from Cross Burgess. Street.* **Right:** *Early*
*Ridgeway 'Handyman' Woodboring Tool Kit, box*
*printing produced by Greenups.* **Facing page:** *Greenup's*
*staff daytrip in 1911.*

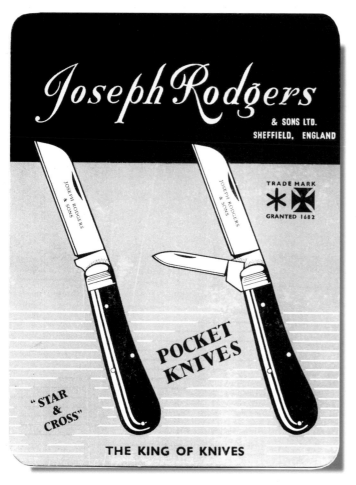

Attractive packaging plus instant product recognition is often what catches the consumer's eye, whether that person is shopping in a large supermarket or in a DIY store, and a pleasing package can be the deciding factor that persuades a customer to actually buy the goods. Greenups' policy has long been to offer their clients a range of packaging designs that deliberately aims to boost the sale of a particular product, and they are able to tailor make cartons in a wide range of styles and sizes. They are asked to provide specialist packaging for such products as tools, lamp bulbs, pet foods, pens, batteries, sharp knives and packs of polythene bags on a roll.

Because the products are so diverse in type, shape, size and requirement, the design of cartons and packaging therefore needs careful consideration from many angles, and the company are often required to apply their considerable expertise to many complicated projects that other companies will not even consider. Whatever the requirement, Greenups undertake to rise to the challenge.

Sales often hang on the style of packaging given to a product, for example stylish and luxurious packaging would be the key selling point of products such as perfumes, lingerie and cosmetics. On the other hand, sometimes the

practical aspect of packaging a certain product needs to be considered, such as the protection from sharp edges that needs to be incorporated into packaging for a saw or a kitchen knife. On occasions it is the actual finish of a package that is a priority, such as the production of moisture proof packs for products like pizza. Their specialist equipment includes a skin coating machine and hot air drying equipment - a necessity as the firm's innovative packaging includes the use of cartons, vacuum formed blister cards, window cartons, hanging cards, skin pack boards and printed wallets. However demanding the challenge, Greenups will find a solution to the problem.

The world's most advanced printing technology is used for Greenups products. After the sixth colour is printed, their Roland 700 press applies a finishing coat of varnish, printing and sealing the package in one pass. This commitment to a continual investment in the latest technology is only one of the factors that have contributed to the success of the company. Greenups have a declared policy of being there to actively help their customers in selling their products, and such prestigious names as Stanley Tools, Spear and Jackson, Boots the Chemist, Wisdom Toothbrushes, Berol and Swann Morton figure on their list of clients.

Asked what factor gives the company the edge with their competitors (who number many!) they might reply, their longest serving member of staff, Alec Hagyard, who joined the company in 1954.

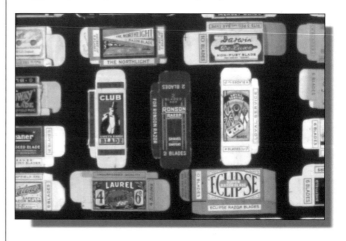

*Top: Joseph Rodgers, pocket knives, an example of a print produced by Greenups at the early part of the century.*
*Above: Further examples of Greenups packaging - 1930's razor blade cartons.*

Since then he has continued to give Greenups Packaging and their clients one hundred percent of his considerable experience and know how. Mr Hagyard is typical of the company's trained workforce - Greenups employ more than 120 people, and their aim is to continue to maintain their commitment to excellence. The firm's highly trained team of customer liaison staff maintain a close involvement with customers and offers an all round customer service that addresses complicated problems and provides clients with innovative solutions.

As packaging is often responsible for a crucial part of its customers' production process, speed is often of the essence, and from the moment an order is received by the staff in the Sales Office and the Production Department consulted, the firm's prompt personal service gives clients a guarantee that their order will be delivered on time and on budget.

Since the early 1980s Greenups have invested heavily in keeping abreast of the latest technology and up to date equipment. Computer Aided Design, for example, enables ideas to be quickly designed and developed so that packs can be manufactured, cut, folded and glued speedily and efficiently. The process also means that the entire production can be accomplished in house, and even short runs of three to four thousand can be produced for a customer.

The aim of the company is to go forward into the coming millennium maintaining the same commitment to long term investment; investment that will ensure that in the years to come Greenups Packaging will still be there to meet every future need of their customers.

*Above and Below:* World War Two damage to the Wellington Steel Factory.

# Modern techniques - but the eye of the craftsman

The Sheffield company, Arkote Limited, gets its name from a contraction of the name of its parent company. A R Heathcote & Company which was formed by Albert Reaney Heathcote in 1881 and operated from Dacre Street in the Park district of Sheffield which is where the Parkhill flats now stand.

Mr Heathcote had previously been a chisel and edge tool manufacturer. The first sale of tobacco knives was recorded on April 5th 1881 to W D & H O Wills for the sum of £24 17s. From that time the firm supplied knives to manufacturers of tobacco cutting machines. At the same time the company was selling some edge tools and, in addition, had a flourishing business in grindstones, quarried at Ackworth, near Pontefract.

The business prospered until the First World War, but then declined. In August 1919, the owner, A R Heathcote, then 75 years of age, took Mr Percy F Osborne into partnership and a limited company was formed. Mr Heathcote as chairman and Mr Osborne, who had been works' manager for J Riley Carr, as managing director. Following Mr Heathcote's death in 1941, at the age of 97, Mr Osborne became sole owner of the company and assumed the chairmanship.

In the period between the two World Wars the company's activities had undergone a change. The edge tool business had finally disappeared and now the main activity was the manufacture of knives for the tobacco industry. The company had extended its activities into the manufacture of machine knives for the paper, metal-working and woodworking industries.

In March 1934 a new factory was opened in Sydney Street, Sylvester Gardens, P S Osborne joined the company in the same year, followed by John Osborne in 1939. During the War, of course, the products of the company were essential to the war effort. In addition to knives, the company also manufactured Primer Cap Plates, (PCPs which were used in the manufacture of percussion caps for cartridges,) and tank turret doors which were supplied to Vauxhall Motors.

The company continued to expand and diversify and after the war, the demand for its products was such that, by 1950, it had become necessary to buy more manufacturing space. In the meantime, there had been a revolutionary change in the method of cutting tobacco. This involved a totally different type of knives being used, which, in turn meant the need for new machinery and new methods of production.

In June 1950, therefore, Arkote was formed. It began operations at a factory in the Hope Valley and continued there until 1955.

When because it was difficult to recruit local labour, production was moved back to Sheffield. There Arkote produced the modern types of tobacco cutting knives which were still marketed under the old and respected name, of Heathcote. Although, since the inauguration of Arkote, the sale of its products to certain customers had been effected on a direct basis.

In November 1961, P F Osborne sadly died. Sidney Osborne succeeded him as Chairman of A R Heathcote, whilst John Osborne became Chairman & managing director of Arkote.

*Below: Automatic polishing department.*
*Facing page: P. F Osborne better known as Percy, father of chairman, John Osborne.*

entity under the direction of John Osborne and Percy Osborne's grandson, Joe Truelove. Mr Truelove was educated in Zimbabwe, where he obtained an Agricultural degree and subsequently he was involved in tobacco farming until, for medical reasons he was compelled to return to England.

In 1969 A R Heathcote & Company was sold to Balfour Darwins Limited, after which it had various owners as the Sheffield steel industry was reorganised. It finally ceased manufacturing some years ago.

By that time, it had been decided to consolidate production and sales by concentrating all activities connected with the tobacco industry at Arkote whilst A R Heathcote took over all the companies' other products.

In January 1962 Arkote finally moved into its present premises at Hawk Works, Mary Street where it operated there as an entirely separate

In 1979 Arkote purchased Samuel Staniforth Limited, a very old-established Sheffield cutlery forge and although the forge was closed some years ago the company is now one of the main manufacturers of trade knives used in the catering and meat industries.

After a very serious fire at Hawk works in 1985, the efforts made by the whole workforce of Arkote to get production restarted illustrates the great corporate spirit of the whole concern. No customers were let down and indeed, very few were aware how near Arkote had been to disaster. Many of the staff have very long service records and it has been said 'Arkote workers don't leave, they retire.'

The present factory utilising cold rolled alloy steel, and having continuous electric furnaces and automatic grinding and polishing equipment is a far cry from the early production methods. Strict quality control throughout all processes ensures consistency in size, temper and finish, so that Arkote products are recognised everywhere for their trouble-free performance and built-in efficiency.

Although modern techniques play an important part in the Arkote production programme, the eye and hand of the craftsman remain vital in determining the quality of the finished product.

*Below: Heat treatment department.*
*Facing page top: Directors from left to right are Sidney Osborne, John Osborne and Joe Truelove.*
*Facing page bottom: Samuel Staniforths circa 1900.*

# Vehicle bodybuilders

The story of Shefflex begins with two young British aristocrats with money, a sense of adventure and the ambition to produce the best car in the world.

One was a son of Lord Llangattock who met a Manchester electrician, turned automotive engineer and formed a partnership. The two men opened a brand new factory in Derby and gave the car it produced the joint surnames of the partners, Rolls and Royce!

The other was Earl Fitzwilliam, a seventh earl in his own right, with a fondness for steam locomotives. He commissioned an already highly respected figure from the British Daimler Company to design his motoring master-piece and, in 1906, had a motor works constructed at Tinsley, on the road between Sheffield and Rotherham, at a cost of £1,000. Its name, Sheffield-Simplex, was a compound one, taking in the name of a famous steel manufacturing town and 'Simplex' was meant to suggest ease of driving.

During the Great War the motor works made munitions, including aero engines and the smaller Commer trucks. This latter opportunity came through Commer and Sheffield Simplex having common directors.

30/50 B.H.P.
High Speed Diesel Oil Engine Chassis

SHEFFLEX

BRITISH COMMERCIAL VEHICLE

Three-Ton Standard Lorry

A MEDIUM WEIGHT 3 TONNER
fitted with the
PETTER A.C.E. ENGINE
"An Outstanding Achievement"

"Tens of Thousands of users all over the World testify to the satisfaction which the Petter two cycle heavy oil engines have given them."

Chassis Price £775 Ex Works

SHEFFLEX MOTORS LIMITED
TINSLEY SHEFFIELD

Unfortunately this second company slid into obscurity after the 1920 Motor Show. It was their final fling at the luxury market and it failed to find enough buyers to make production worthwhile.

Meanwhile, when the post-war demand for new lorries evaporated Commer too was in serious difficulties. The receiver cancelled Commer's contract with Sheffield Simplex who were left with dozens of lorries in various states of assembly. When these were finished, they were sold with a hurriedly designed 'Shefflex' badge and they were disposed of to a war surplus dealer who found a ready market for them.

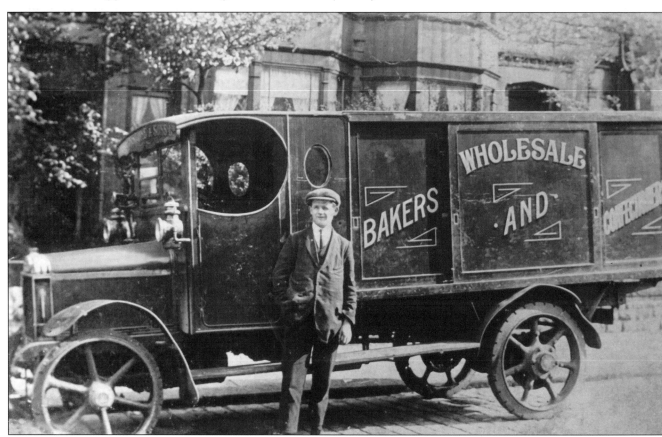

This dealer, R A Johnstone of Tinsley, was also a local garage owner and haulage contractor. After a certain number of difficulties, he managed to acquire the Shefflex name from the defunct Sheffield-Simplex in 1926, when he founded the shefflex Motor Company.

Initially, sales were purely local, but a few agents were appointed around the country, and, in 1928, Kennings took over the whole northern territory.

In 1929 versions of the basic model were given semi-forward control to increase body space and 50 cwt models were announced at Shefflex's first visit to an Olympia show that year. During 1930 Dorman engines gradually ousted the Commer-type units. The following year saw a further development, a six ton articulated lorry with Ryburn trailer.

Sales were falling, partly because of the Depression and partly because of competition from the new mass-produced mid-weight vehicles such as Bedfords. It might well have been the end of the valiant little firm if it had not been for a meeting of its management with a Polish Jew who had changed his name to John Sherwood. whilst acting as Continental representative for Guy, Mr Sherwood had encountered the Faun refuse compaction system. This was initially made in England for Sherwoods by Shefflex. The first was ready for Sheffield in 1934 on an Electricar six wheel chassis. Then, in 1935 came a chassis built by Shefflex themselves.

Shefflex Ltd became the company title in 1938 when it moved its premises to Rutland Street. Mr Sherwood was the agent and about two dozen municipal vehicles were built before war intervened.

After the war, Shefflex Ltd concentrated on municipal bodywork and soon became general bodybuilders.

*Above: From the early part of the century an example of Shefflex trucks for commercial business.*
*Left: Tom Grove fueling up a new vehicle on a road test in 1935.*
*Facing page above: An early advertisement of Shefflex commercial vehicles.*
*Facing page bottom: A 1924 Shefflex 30/40 model for William Gunstones & Son, Sheffield.*

At the end of the second world war after fulfiling, various WD contracts the company returned to its pre war activity which was the manufacture of refuse collection bodywork on standard commercial vehicle chassis, unique to the Shefflex design was the patented "dustless hood" system which was a hinged and sealed hood and framework which when fitted to an enclosed refuse collection body enabled the operator to discharge a standard galvanised dustbin of the time, full of fine ash from a coal fire, into the vehicle body without coming into contact with the contents, this was a tremendous advantage over other competitor manufacturers and very good news for the dustbin man.

The company continued along these lines until the late sixties, early seventies when the advent of the smokeless zones became common throughout the country, finally affecting the company in about 1972, The problem was that the Shefflex system relied on the householder burning all their rubbish in the traditional fire grate and having a relatively small bin full of heavy fine ash. The competition had meanwhile been developing alternative types of refuse collection vehicles for other parts of an already smokeless zoned countryside, this involved high volume bodywork with very efficient Internal compactors to reduce the volume of what was now a dustbin and several bags full of paper, plastic and general waste which could not now be burned on the traditional grate and as The

Sheffield City Council Cleansing Dept had become their last customer for the dustless hood system the company went into decline., belatedly attempting to develop its own version of a compactor in the middle seventies. This venture failed and the company finally pulled out of the refuse collector, manufacturing business in 1974, various contracts were undertaken over the next three years but it was a steady decline to a workforce of 3 by 1977.

The current era of the "Shefflex Story" began in November 1977 when William Barrott a Sheffield businessman involved in the motor trade operating a very successful new and used car sales dealership and a specialised vintage car, restoration business got together with Michael Daniel a sales engineer working for a local vehicle body manufacturer. The company was relaunched as a general purpose vehicle bodybuilder, manufacturing all types of bodywork from small platform bodies to 40' articulated trailers, the business grew to employing over, 25 craftsmen by the

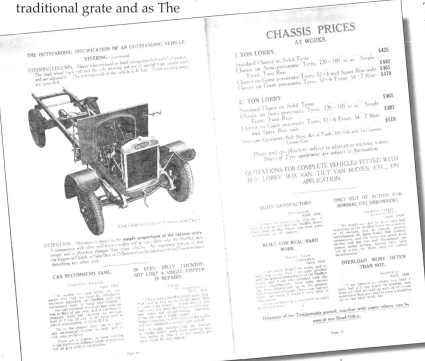

*Above: Shefflex bodywork on an Electricar six wheel chassis, 1936.*
*Left: Pages from a Shefflex book stating the Chassis prices from the early days.*

middle eighties, by that time diversification was planned as a means to grow the company and to this end a small steel fabrication company called Lem & Unwin was purchased from the 2 retiring owners George Lem & Ron Unwin and a new 27000 sq. ft of production space purchased at the present site , By 1990 the steel fabrication division of the company accounted for a majority share of the company turnover and the decision taken to pull out of general vehicle bodybuilding and concentrate the company resources into steel fabrication.

A significant turning point in the companies development occurred in 1991 when Shefflex Ltd purchased the manufacturing division of Towsure ltd, one of the UK's largest distributors of vehicle towing equipment, The workforce was boosted to 40 and production of the Towsure range of towbars began at the end of 1991, Bill Barrott retired from the company in 1991 and now concentrates his efforts on his widely acclaimed vintage car restoration business which has

clients world wide. Shefflex Ltd is now owned and run by Mike Daniel and his wife and son Chris.

Development of the Towsure range along with a committed expansion plan by Towsure Ltd who retained the sole agency for the towbar range, and who carry out all the marketing and nationwide sales for the wide range of over 300 different towbar models and the recently introduced regulation EC94/20 regarding the manufacture and fatigue testing of all new towbar design which increases the complexity and manufacturing content of all new products along with the concentrated sales efforts of our client Towsure has helped increase the workforce to over 70 in 1998.

The company's roots in Vehicle bodybuilding and general fabrication have not been totally abandoned and a small nucleus of 12 employees continue the tradition of specialist jobs having recently completed the manufacture and installation of a large racking and storage contract for a multinational company and the conversion of a specialised vehicle complete with a large rear mounted crane and tyre handling equipment including compressor and tooling required to service the tyres of huge earth moving equipment in the heart of Africa.

*Above: Shefflex refuse collection bodywork on an Electricar HGV chassis in 1938.*
*Left: Leyland daf chassis cab with specialised refuse collection body for Sheffield council. Dated 1985.*

# From tea sets to temperature

Henry Land had been a commercial traveller before he married and settled down. He needed a steady job, but nevertheless in 1845 he set up in business, establishing a company to manufacture Britannia metal tableware.

He started up his traditional Sheffield business in premises in Arundel Street, later diversifying into electroplated silverware and pewter. His five sons followed him into the business. Sadly, when his wife Elizabeth died Henry began to drink heavily, and he neglected the business. His fourth son Tom had to start again virtually from scratch. Tom's courage and determination helped to get the business back on its feet, and soon Land's was prospering.

Tom's son Frank contributed to the success when he joined the company, and around the turn of the century they built new premises in Queens Road. The factory was in use until 1962, when expansion led to the current site being bought in Dronfield. Land's suffered their setbacks during World War One, as many businesses did, and workers being called up meant a shortage of labour. But Land's survived, and played their part in the war effort, manufacturing fuse bodies for shells.

After the war it was necessary to retrain the returning workers in the electro-plate trade.    At the same time, however, the fashion in silver-plated tableware was changing; domestic servants were becoming a thing of the past - and silver plated teasets had to be cleaned regularly!

The company changed direction and began to manufacture pewter.

Frank's son Tom, who in 1935 had gained a degree in physics from Cambridge University, went into the business. When war broke out once again in 1939

Tom joined the Territorial Army in the Artillery. But physicists were too valuable to the country to be used as gunners; Tom was offered a job in the steel industry, working on the measurement of temperature in steel. He loved the work, and decided that this was what he wanted to do for the rest of his life.

After the war, in 1947 Frank and Tom Land used their electroplate and pewter business to fund the startup of a new business, Land Pyrometers.

The manufacture of industrial thermometers for the steel industry was a job that Tom could get his teeth into and use his talents to the full. They ordered some equipment and engaged a couple of men and a girl to do the typing, and they were in business.

The new business grew fast, and the pewter company was eventually sold. The year 1959-60 produced a profit of more than £25,000, a figure that increased year by year.

Land Pyrometers started out by supplying infrared non contact thermometers and thermocouples, mainly to the steel industry. As the firm expanded they went into the glass industry - and in fact into any process that called for the measurement of temperature. With the aim of producing instruments that were not only of high quality but were user-friendly, the business took off. They expanded internationally, forming an American subsidiary in 1970.

With the power generating industry in mind, and using their existing technology the company branched out into another new field in the late

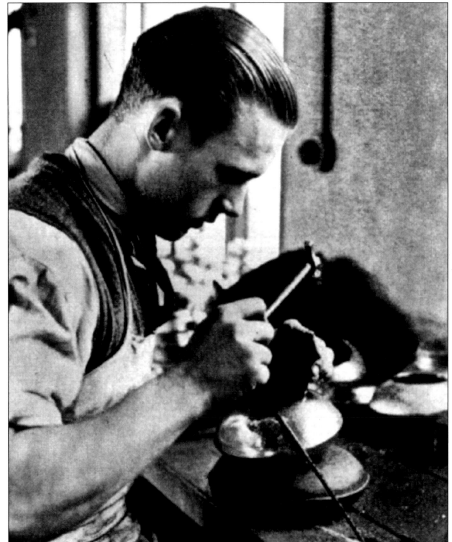

staff and distributors. Their workforce is very committed, with large numbers of long service employees and a very low staff turnover - a product of Land's policy of providing the very best possible working conditions for their workforce. 1997 saw the celebration of the Company's 50th Anniversary in Instrumentation. An enormous party was arranged at Harewood House, and employees and

1970s, monitoring the efficiency of combustion processes in large boilers.

By the early 1980's the company had three divisions, Land Pyrometers, selling thermocouples to the steel and foundry industry (later sold to a German-owned company), Land Combustion, selling combustion monitoring equipment and Land Infrared, selling infrared thermometers to a wide variety of industries.

In 1977 Tom's daughter Jasmine Harfoot joined the company - the fifth generation member of the Land family, and she is the current Group Managing Director. Tom Land is the current Chairman. The past ten years have seen subsidiaries opened in France, Germany, Italy, Poland and Japan. The global scale of the company means that main competitors are from America, Germany and Japan. All the product development takes place in Dronfield, however, and most of the products are still manufactured there. The plant has around 200 employees.

Land's principles have always leaned towards a commitment to staying at the forefront of technology, and the company spends significant amounts on product development. Dedicated also to customer care, they concentrate on training

pensioners from Britain and overseas had the opportunity to get to know colleagues from around the world.

Land Instruments International has plans for the future that include more of the same - progress, advancement and growth in the global market place in the 21$^{st}$ Century.

*Facing page top:* The Product Development Laboratory *in 1969.* **Facing page bottom:** *A view of Colonial Works, Queens Road about 1950.* **Top Left:** *Knocking spots on with a punch and a hammer.* **Top Right:** *The current chairman Tom Land.* **Below:** *New entrance of Land Instruments International Limited 1997.*

# Producing drills since 1913

**D**ormer Tools (Sheffield) Limited was founded as the Sheffield Twist Drill Company in 1913, as a partnership between Mr C W Claxton, who had prior experience in running a twist drill plant, and Mr H A Dormer who was a consulting engineer specialising in railway equipment.

The first workshops consisted of large rooms formerly used as a patent medicine factory in Napier Street, where a total of 20 employees were engaged in the manufacture of twist drills.

In the early days, the firm concentrated chiefly on working customers' own steel into drills and other tools, but there were obvious difficulties in not having complete control over the quality of its products. A decision was taken to obtain the best raw materials to manufacture into tools, rather than continue to use the customers' own materials. A fundamental change in the company's philosophy was reflected in changing the company's name to Sheffield Twist Drill and Steel Company Limited.

In 1915 Dormer became a limited Company. The agent for Holland at that time, W B Diepeveen, of Rotterdam, suggested the use of a windmill with a dormer window as the company trademark. In 1924 the name Dormer became a registered brand name.

FOR SPEED ENDURANCE & PRECISION

SPECIFY

**DORMER**
BRAND

HIGH SPEED STEEL TWIST DRILLS REAMERS, AND END MILLS.

*and in* CARBON STEEL QUALITY "DORMER CARBON"

THE SHEFFIELD TWIST DRILL & STEEL COMPANY LTD.
Phone 24157. SUMMERFIELD ST. SHEFFIELD, 11. 'Grams Proells Sheffield
LONDON OFFICE: 11. QUEEN VICTORIA ST. EC4 Phone City 2660 'Grams Proells, London.

Between 1925-35, although trading conditions were tough, profits were ploughed back into the business, more property was bought in the vicinity and the factory extended. In 1933 the three-storey office block on Napier Street was built.

By 1939 the old buildings had been redesigned or rebuilt and the workforce, now making twist drills and reamers, was 600 strong.

In 1947 Dormer became a public limited company and shares were offered to customers and employees.

In 1950 the Steam temper treatment with its characteristic blue finish was introduced, the company being the first in Europe to introduce this process. Employees now totalled over 1,000.

The London branch office had been trading for several years and, in 1952, branch offices were also opened in Glasgow and Birmingham.

During the next two decades the company expanded its range of products and its

*Above left: Mr H.A. Dormer, managing director, a founder of the company. Above: An early advertisement. Left: An early photo of the works.*

number of employees as more companies were acquired. The first addition in 1953, was Miller Tools in Birmingham, who manufactured milling cutters and other small tools, and in the same year the 'Silver Ring' was introduced onto blue finish tools. Accurate Screw Threads of Hednesford, whose speciality was making jigs and fixtures, was purchased the following year.

In 1957 a new factory was built at Worksop for the production of milling cutters and machine tools for both manufacture and maintenance of engineers' milling cutters.

The sixties saw Dormer acquire Johnson Brothers a tap and die manufacturing plant at Chilwell, Nottingham and by acquiring Napier Steel Limited at Outbridge, enter the field of special high speed steel manufacture.

In 1972 and 1974 respectively Dormer acquired Aldridge Tool & Engineering Company Limited, near Walsall, and William Goode & Company (Engineers) Limited of Nuneaton who became a member of the Group as a shank cutter manufacturer.

In 1975 the Dormer Group became a wholly-owned subsidiary of SKF, a Swedish Multi-National, primarily famous as a bearing manufacturer. The Dormer name was modified to become SKF & Dormer Tools and the companies were gradually added to the SKF Tools division of SKF.

A year of high activity in 1990 involved the purchase of Cofler in Italy, a merger with Gunther in Germany, to create the formation of CTT (Cutting Tool Technology), and the acquisition of assets of union

Butterfield, in the USA. Hillcliff in Sheffield was bought in 1991 and added into the Dormer Group.

In 1992 Sandvik, the company's current owner, acquired CTT from SKF. Sandvik were already producers of other types of cutting tools and Sandvik's investment in CTT and therefore Dormer have benefited both parties. Dormer gains have been specifically in the investment of resources for the development of new products, and in the latest machine tools for manufacturing.

Dormer has a larger dedicated technical salesforce than any other cutting tool manufacturer in the UK. It has 10,000 types of cutting tools in its range, all serviced within 24 hours from a bespoke central warehouse in Europe. This creates greater product availability, improved rates of order fulfillment and the most competitive of delivery times.

By continually pushing back technological barriers, Dormer knows that it is giving its customers the competitive advantage they require to succeed in their own industries.

*Above:* Mr C.W. Claxton, joint managing director who is also a founder of the company. *Below:* Cutting off department and raw material stores.

# Workshop engineering since 1873

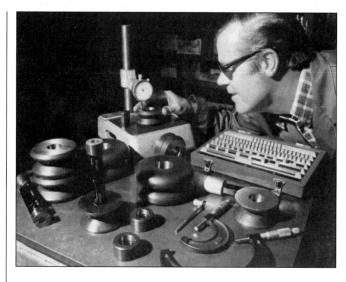

Baker Blower Engineering Company was founded by Sykes and Walter James Travis in 1873. Named after an injection system for open hearth furnaces which the company came to specialise in, Baker Blower was an offshoot of the Saville Street Foundry of which Sykes and Travis were experienced employees. They established the company in a house in Stanley Street, shaded by a plant nursery.

Since then, with each increase in prosperity a new extension has been built on to the house to accommodate new machinery. Now, the house, standing at the centre of the workspace, is home to offices.

Up to the late forties the company made over 100 Baker Blowers which were distributed throughout the UK and Europe. The last was made in 1950 but by this time the company had expanded into repair work and general machining. Much of this was a spin off of their participation in the war effort. when they had machined armour plating for tanks and made shell casing.

In due time Travis's grandson, Walter Harryman-Travis took over.

Baker Blower was by this time a limited company. Under his direction the firm survived the dramatic collapse in the city's steel industry in the sixties by developing its skills and adopting a more sophisticated approach to its stock trade.

Harry Scott, succeeded Travis as Managing Director in 1982, having worked for the company since 1939. Under his regime the firm worked for all the Sheffield steel companies that existed and outlived most of them. Harry Scott attributes this success to the company's long-standing reputation and large customer base.

*Above: An inspector looking at various types of rolls used in different industries.*
*Below: A 'Platt 4B' roll being redressed.*

Since this time trade has vastly improved. Twenty five years ago the company obtained Rolls Royce approval for rectalinear machining. This agreement grew to cover sensitive part approval to critical part approval, which means Baker Blower is now producing parts critical to an aircraft staying aloft. They are proud of this responsibility and do not take it lightly.

The current management is a team of two, Martin Birch and Steve Hill. They have ambitions for the firm but their first consideration is the workers' environment. In this traditional family business the workers are thought of as part of the family.

This new team has produced three consecutive record years, doubling their turnover, after investing in two CNC machines. The company has also become well known for machining titanium alloys and the precision diamond grinding of plasma sprayed products. Together with Plasma Coating Ltd. of Tideswell they are at the forefront of osteopathy. Hydroxlapatite is a hard wearing material that has been found to encourage bone growth. It is therefore being used

to coat artificial hip joints and Baker Blower's most experienced machinists are being used to grind the components of the joint so they are perfectly smooth and can move unhindered.

As the European Community opens up opportunities in the export market, Baker Blower intends to expand in that direction over the next few years.

*Top: A selection of of small roll shapes and types for twist and mill guides.*
*Below: Machined rolls used used in the cold reducing mills.*

# *Going back in time*

In the early 1890s, Harry Ponsford, a skilled silversmith in Sheffield lived with his growing family in a small terraced house in Myrtle Road, Heeley. Desperately needing to earn some extra money he collected payments in the evenings for the local coal merchant. He called in virtually every house both to take orders for coal and to collect monies due.

During this time, customers asked him to obtain household items and this was the start of the Ponsford shop.

The early days were a struggle, silver smithing by day and collecting most evenings, but it was by this enterprise that the family was able to move house, to a slightly larger dwelling each

time. Trading from the back room changed to having a shop in Valley Road. It was by now the twenties and his son and daughter had grown old enough to help him.

Colin, now aged 32, felt that the business would not grow further until it had a main road location. There he could sell the 1930s modern furniture that was such a dramatic change from the tastes of the twenties and before.

Number 581 London Road (still the registered office of the company) forms part of the shop today which now covers from 579-609 London Road with additional buildings stretching back to adjacent streets beyond. The building is steeped in the typical architectural detail of the late 19th century. Recently, considerable renovation work has been sympathetically carried out to restore the building.

*Below: The original shop building in 1932 with Ponsfords at number 581 London Road.* **Bottom:** *The main London Road entrance in 1958 and restored again in 1992.* **Facing Page:** *The full frontage today which is quite a different picture from the first shop of 1932.*

The building has been a source of great interest in the district throughout years of painstaking development. Now finished, it has quite a magical character. Most of the houses round about have either been pulled down or rebuilt less sympathetically than the Ponsford-owned property. This has been carefully preserved and the Victorian shop front has been restored. Every time improvement takes place some fresh piece of history is unearthed.

Perhaps the fabric of the building is old but the company is very much youthful in outlook and alive. It has earned and maintained for many years its status as one of the best furniture shops in the country. The spectrum of furniture, carpets and beds is the envy of many outside companies and it is still very much a family company - one of the few to survive to the fourth generation.

If your interests are historic, if you are inquisitive or determined to see some of the finest goods on offer, find the time to visit the Ponsford store. A large car park and gardens have been built behind the store to bring present day facilities to the customer. The standards of service and attention maintain true old fashioned values. There are very few businesses that have survived the transitions over the years and it is exciting to see this company go from strength to strength.

*Top: The first van owned by the company. There is still at the shop the traditional Victorian barrow that many goods were delivered on to the immediate locality but the van, obviously, gave the company much wider opportunities. Bottom: Sympathetic building work behind the premises which now extend back to the side roads complete the Coronation Street architecture. The cobbles were reclaimed from the yard area that has now been converted into showrooms and beyond is the car park for 50 cars.*

# The company which grew with its products

Ernest H Hill Ltd was established in Sheffield in 1841 as an engineering and manufacturing company. Over the years the company has designed and manufactured a comprehensive range of fluid transfer equipment, meeting customers' changing requirements on a world-wide basis.

For many years, however, they manufactured only garden syringes. In 1888 the first tyre pumps in the world were made for Dunlop and afterwards the company's range of products greatly extended.

The business had been started originally by a man named Arthur Smith and was purchased on behalf of Ernest Hill in 1917. Mr Hill had been born in Attercliffe and apprenticed as a silver chaser. His son Ernest Henry came into the business and, by 1932 Ernest Henry and Harold Hill had become joint managing directors. Harold, however, felt his future was elsewhere and he relinquished his shares.

During the period of the First World War, until 1920, Mr Hill spent much time on the study of non ferrous metallurgy, becoming Associate Metallurgist of Sheffield University. He presented that university with £100 to provide an annual award for a metallurgy student.

An extension of 36,000 square feet was built in the late thirties. It comprised five floors, including new offices, machine and assembling shops, all with modern (for then) layout designed to speed up production.

**Right:** *Air-raid precautions equipment leaflet, which was published in co-operation with the Home Office during World War 2.*

**Below:** *Hill created the originally built Sheffield Motor Co, 1901-2. Premises acquired about 1916. The Sheffield Motor Co, was established here, Archibald Barnes being managing director. Business moved to new building in 1904 and this part over. E.H.H. machine shop burnt down february 26th 1909.*

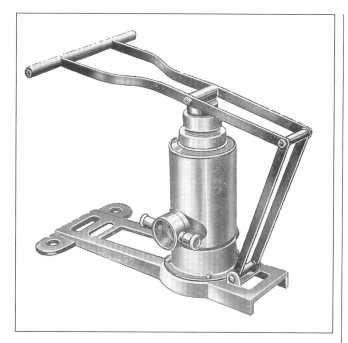

The company incorporated its own Tube Mill for brass and copper tube, foundries for brass, gunmetal and aluminium castings, plating shop for nickel, chrome, cadmium and copper plating and box making and printing plant.

The products at this time comprised a wide range of sprayers for paint, horticultural and agricultural purposes and disinfecting. The firm also produced hand operated air and water pumps, motor accessories, veterinary pumps, pumps for ARP purposes and many other articles to special specifications.

By 1936 the business had premises in Fitzwilliam Street, Broomhall Street, Broomspring

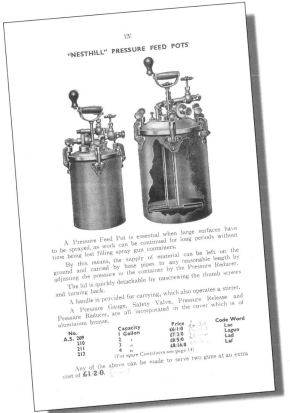

10

## "NESTHILL" AEROSPRAYER No. 45/50

For attaching to compressors which have no storage tank i.e. small garage compressor.

The storage tank smooths out any pulsations from the compressor tank along with the air drier removes any oil or water. A pressure gauge is fitted and a blow off valve so that if the compressor provides more air than the gun requires, no harm results.

The spray gun is the "NESTHILL" Champion as fitted to the air drier illustrated on page 9 and will give excellent service enabling all kinds of jobs to be undertaken.

No. A.S. 45/50 Aerosprayer     £6 16 0     Code Word Kvestor
(with 10 feet of Rubber Hose)

Lane, Cavendish Street, Hodgeson Street and Bath Street

During the Second World War Hill produced equipment designed and produced in close co-operation with the Home Office including a variety of pumps and other fire fighting equipment and canvas fire buckets. During the Sheffield Blitz in December 1940 the firm had suffered considerable damage. A bomb had fallen into the Tube Mill and blown it out completely and there was much damage done to other buildings. Fortunately, the workers on the shift at the time, busy in the basement, continued unharmed. The Hill workers were, in the main, considered to be in reserved occupations and so there were few staffing problems though supplies of materials were controlled.

After the war, orders flooded in. The emergency rebuilding done during the war was replaced by a

*Above left: Two man manual pump for dealing with fires it could output 12 gallons per minute at 30 lbs.*
*Above right: Aerosprayer, for attaching to compressors which have no storage tank, i.e. small garage compressor. This page is also taken from 'Paint by Power'.*
*Left: "Nesthill" Pressure feed pots, for spraying large surfaces. This page is from Nesthills 'Paint by Power' book which dates back to the 1960's.*

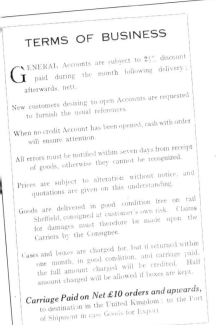

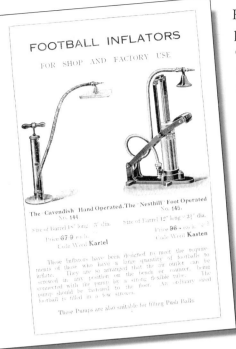

FOOTBALL INFLATORS

FOR SHOP AND FACTORY USE

The Cavendish Hand Operated. No. 144. Size of Barrel 18″ long 3″ dia. Price 67 9 each. Code Word **Kartel**

The Nesthill Foot Operated No. 145. Size of Barrel 12″ long 3½″ dia. Price 96 each. Code Word **Kasten**

Fitzwilliam Street to the present premises. Here the company continues to supply the petroleum and oil industry, using all the most modern technology. Recently there has been a move into the manufacture pumps for chemicals for a worldwide market. The company designed and manufactured a jet engine inhibitor rig for jets working in hostile environments. It is interesting that this piece of high tech equipment is based on the principle of the old Hills Horticultural spray. Ernest Hill Ltd has new customers in the modern industrial world but it remains loyal to the old ones too. When Iran bought from the Rootes Group the license to build Hillman Hunters in Iran, under the name 'Pecan', Hill supplies him with hose clips. Since the Iranian company still produces the Pecan, Ernest Hill Ltd still supplies the hose clips.

With customers old and new, this company seems set to embark on a further successful 150 years' trading.

permanent new press shop and other new buildings were put up, the programme being completed in 1950.

At this time, goods were illustrated in a two colour art catalogue, available to customers on request. The range of goods included driving mirrors, especially those for buses and trucks, a variety of syringes, pump connectors, sprayers and hose clips as well as pumps.

In 1991, the present managing director, Mr Hewins, joined the company and a move was made from

*Above:* Page from Nesthill's booklet of football inflators.
*Below:* Ernest Hill, Beta Works, Fitzwilliam Street Branch. The now defunct workings.

# ACKNOWLEDGMENTS

SHEFFIELD CENTRAL LIBRARY: LOCAL STUDIES

SHEFFIELD FIRE AND POLICE MUSEUM

MRS AILEEN NORTH

MR ERNEST OXLEY